THE ST GEORGE HOTEL BAR

THE ST GEORGE HOTEL BAR

SAÏD K. ABURISH

BLOOMSBURY

First published in Great Britain 1989

Copyright © 1989 by Saïd K. Aburish

Bloomsbury Publishing Ltd, 2 Soho Square, London W1V 5DE

A CIP catalogue record for this book
is available from the British Library

ISBN 0-7475-0221-8

Typeset by Hewer Text Composition Services, Edinburgh
Printed and bound in Great Britain by Richard Clay Ltd, Bungay, Suffolk

FOR CHARLA
AND FOR LAURA MOLTEDO

CONTENTS

	Introduction	1
1	The Centre of the Centre of the Middle East	3
2	A Day in the Life of the St George Hotel Bar	15
3	The First Draft of History – St George Hotel Bar Version	35
4	The Truth Emerges	52
5	The Coup That Never Was	65
6	Spies and Friends – Kim Philby	75
7	Spies and Friends – the CIA and Others	86
8	It's a Dirty Game, it's a Deadly Game	96
9	Yes, Mr Getty	109
10	A Bribe as Big as the St George	118
11	Rogues	127
12	Between the Prince and the Prime Minister	141
13	Strange Bedfellows	148
14	Careless Eden? Sceptical Nasser?	155
15	Green with Money	163
16	Sisters of Men	177
17	A World No More	188
18	Lebanon Finale – the Beginning of Terror	201
	Index	211

INTRODUCTION

I like to think that the books I write are a labour of love. This attitude helps me overcome the difficulties inherent in writing, including the all-important and often dislocating factor of loneliness. I maintained this positive approach throughout the research for and the writing of this book, and I began referring to it as 'a fun project'. I am delighted to report that it has remained that way and that I am as happy with the finished product as I was with the original idea.

This is a book about espionage, journalistic and business activities which took place at the St George Hotel* bar in Beirut over a period of twenty years, activities which shaped – and which continue to influence – the contemporary Middle East, events similar to the arms sales negotiations which provoked the Irangate scandal, the 1988 twenty-billion-dollar Saudi Arabian-UK defence deal and the continued insistence of the Western press on overlooking the crimes of 'our friends'. There are no apologies to make and no turgid explanations to offer. Two simple matters deserve mention: dividing the book into sections has created minor difficulties as to where and under which heading each story belongs; and I have had to take extra care to avoid either harming innocent people or writing anything libellous. That's all.

First, when a story encompasses more than one sphere of activity, involving both journalism and espionage or both business and politics, for instance – as most of them do – I have relied on my own judgement to decide where it belongs,

* The French name, Hôtel Saint-Georges, has been anglicized in this book.

1

i.e., whether it relates more to one realm than to the other. Inevitably some readers will disagree with my placement of some stories; but such matters could be argued for ever. Second, damage to people and their reputations has been avoided wherever possible, and strictly personal elements of a story which have little or no relevance to the main theme have not been included. To state it crudely, I do not care who slept with whom, where or when. Finally, exposures of the type presented in this book often invite libel action and, while the ensuing publicity might boost sales, I would prefer to direct my energies towards writing another book than towards defending this one. I am confident that what I have reported has been checked and rechecked and represents what actually happened. On those occasions when I have used initials or changed dates, it has been to avoid hurt and harm to others, not to protect myself.

Thanks are due to a large number of people, sixteen of whom have requested that their names be withheld. The others, in order of date of interview or exchange of letters, are: Khaldoun Solh, Raymond Edde, Jean Bertolet, Salim Nassar, Hanna Ghossun, Ali Bitar, Mohammad Mseitif, Myrna Bustani, Paul and Lorice Parker, John and Vanya Cooley, Gavin Scott, Tony Brown, Erik de Mauney, Ralph and Molly Izzard, Gavin Young, Murray Gart, John Bulloch, Abu Saïd, Anthony Cavendish, Bill MacLaughlin, Jonathan Randall, David Ignatius, Karsten Prager, John Chancellor, John Steinbreader and Sheikh Najib Allumedine.

Others whose help has taken the form of encouragement and valuable advice are David Reynolds, my editor at Bloomsbury, John Lawton, Marione (Brookie) Stapelbroek, Mary Chamberlain, my brother Wagih and sister-in-law Eileen, and Shelly and Daphne Borkum.

It is my hope that people will enjoy reading this book as much as I have enjoyed writing it.

1
THE CENTRE
OF THE CENTRE
OF THE MIDDLE EAST

At one p.m. on 23 January 1963 Kim Philby walked into the St George Hotel bar, sat down at his regular table and had his customary five or six afternoon drinks. His perfunctory goodbyes when he left shortly before three suggested that he would be back the next day, as usual. But Philby vanished from Beirut that very evening and the bar staff never saw 'Mr Keem' or 'Mr Pheelby' again. Even as I write, investigations are under way to determine if Philby in fact returned to Beirut after his defection, whether to visit the grave of his famous Orientalist father or to 'take care of' an untidy bank account whose discovery would have revealed much about the famous spy's activities in the Middle East.

Months afterwards, James Russell Barracks, an agent of the US Central Intelligence Agency (CIA), openly questioned the bar staff and various habitués about Kim's behaviour on the day he disappeared. Disappointed to learn that Philby had acted normally, Barracks exhaled a deep sigh of frustration. 'How the hell did he do it? How did he get away?' Weeks later, Barracks was mysteriously murdered in far-off Nigeria.

Abu Saïd of *Time* magazine was among those crudely questioned by Barracks. Although Abu Saïd responded to the impromptu CIA interrogation with a non-committal shrug of the shoulders, he was seething inside. A week earlier, he had seen a document describing how Philby had left Beirut. But Abu Saïd's source had changed his mind and the document had disappeared. Was he simply afraid, or did someone, somewhere, order the tipster to suppress or destroy the evidence? The answer is unknown to this day.

All that Kim Philby, Jim Barracks and Abu Saïd had in common was the St George Hotel bar.

Paraphrasing Ernest Hemingway has never been an easy business, but for those of us lucky enough to have known the St George Hotel bar during the fifties, sixties and seventies, life will never be the same again; the bar will always be with us, an invisible, hallowed component of our existence which we celebrate wherever we may be.

For us, this book is an elegy, a pleasant remembrance of a unique place and atmosphere which contributed to the way we are and whose memory continues to shape our world-view. As for those who never knew it, including the many who heard second-hand reports, I hope that this book will acquaint them with this singular spot and its special ambience and I suffer the trepidation of someone who is about to introduce a valued friend, imbued with all the reverent affection that accompanies such an act.

But why should anyone write a book about what is, after all, just a bar? What is it that makes me, and others who knew it, remember the place so fondly, as something more than just another setting for the colourful lives of international bar flies? The simple answer is that we are unlikely to see another place like the St George Hotel bar ever again; its mix of ingredients cannot be reproduced.

In 1973, *Fortune* magazine featured the St George Hotel bar in an article on the top seven hotel bars in the world which serve as centres for international businessmen, emphasizing its 'tranquility, comfortable surroundings, generously mixed drinks and competent, unobtrusive service'. This description, though true, paints only part of the bigger picture. Two important features made Beirut's St George Hotel bar stand out from the others: its regular clientele included journalists, spies, Arab politicians, Lebanese chieftains and foreign diplomats, as well as international businessmen, and, unlike the bars of London, Paris, New York and elsewhere, it had no competition, no substitute. Its singleness of atmosphere was absolute.

This interaction of journalism, international business and espionage in the turbulent context of local Lebanese and regional Arab politics created an extraordinary milieu. The players included J. Paul Getty and Daniel Ludwig, Kim Philby and Archie Roosevelt, Joe Alsop and Sefton Delmer – every name in the annals of Middle Eastern politics, and the name of the game – reporting, exploiting, manipulating and controlling the Middle East. A rare phenomenon, indeed. Visiting the St George Hotel bar was like going to one of the most beautiful and best-run theatres in the world to watch Olivier, Gielgud and Richardson perform Shakespeare.

Even those habitués untouched by fame were seasoned men of the world for whom money, style and power were familiar commodities. As a result, the bar towered above all places of its type, the way Shepherds in Cairo and the Athene Palace in Bucharest did during the Second World War. The reality of the St George Hotel bar surpassed any thriller writer's most improbable invention; its appealing and mysterious world witnessed revelations more sordid than any tabloid newspaper headlines.

Jean Bertolet, the hotel's general manager from 1961 to 1969, speaks nostalgically of 'a unique, once-a-century happening. I felt as if my clients were running the Middle East, occasionally the world.' Myrna Bustani, part-owner of the hotel, one-time Lebanese member of parliament and chairwoman of the leading international company Contracting and Trading (CAT), refuses to compare the bar with any other place: 'No, no, no . . . please, there is no place like it . . . perhaps The Gritti in Venice but not quite, no no.'

One great strength of the St George Hotel bar was its location in Beirut, then the centre of the Middle East and a cosmopolitan city experiencing its heyday. Geographically and historically Beirut has been the gateway through which people, goods and ideas passed to and from Arabia proper since Phoenician times. Other cities have competed for this honour: Tyre, Sidon and Acre in ancient times and, more recently, Haifa and Jaffa. But in this century, political and economic developments in the region eliminated other likely contenders. By the early fifties, Beirut reigned supreme as the crossroads where East and West met to shape the future of the lands beyond, the Middle East.

Three major happenings aided Beirut's elevation to unrivalled international pre-eminence. The Israeli occupation of Jaffa and Haifa following the 1948 Arab-Israeli War ruled them out as regional harbours and eliminated Palestine as an oil outlet to the Mediterranean. When Nasser gained control of Egypt in 1952, his socialist outlook precluded Cairo's development as a competitor to Beirut. Finally, the oil wealth of the Middle East required a sophisticated commercial and banking centre. These regional factors transformed the Middle East into an arena of superpower contention, a battleground for propagandists and spies, and Beirut at its centre into a sort of latter-day Athens and a playground for the Arab world. And this it remained until 1975 and the advent of the Lebanese civil war – euphemistically known as 'The Troubles' – which haunts and hounds us to this day.

But Beirut's ascent to eminence owed as much to what might be called the Lebanese factor as it did to wider regional forces. Both the Lebanese people and government rose to the challenge of being the centre of the Middle East instinctively and most effectively. Trading, if not outright wheeling and dealing, is second nature to most Lebanese, but it is only fair to record the energy which they applied to realize the opportunity which confronted them. They learned English in addition to the French they had already acquired, and often used both languages interchangeably with great wit. They opened excellent restaurants and nightclubs, built modern apartment buildings and foreign community schools, provided domestic help and, above all, received foreigners with open arms (some even insisting on the Arab embrace for greeting reluctant Westerners). The Lebanese government, committed to Beirut's emerging new rôle as 'the capital of the Middle East', built an international airport and a magnificent casino, expanded and modernized the city's communication facilities and created one of the best-run airlines in the world, aptly named Middle East Airlines. The far-sighted member of parliament Raymond Edde proposed Swiss-style banking security laws which were enacted even though some of his colleagues could not fathom their meaning, knowing only that such legislation would help Beirut's business. (Some Moslem deputies opposed the measure because it contradicted the Koranic command 'to speak of wealth'.)

As its capital evolved into an international business centre, democratic, self-confident Lebanon avoided taking sides or any extreme position in the political conflicts which racked the region. For a long time its border with Israel remained unprotected. Lebanon's commitment to neutrality not only enhanced Beirut's acceptability as a regional business centre, but also made it a political centre. Refugees from the neighbouring countries of Iraq, Syria, Jordan, Egypt and others came to Beirut because it was near, Arab and free – a place, unlike their dictatorial homes, where they could continue their activities. For this reason, Beirut's foreign embassies had commercial and political duties which were regional in nature, transcending their representational function to the Lebanese government.

As a commercial centre and a home for the Middle East's political exiles, Beirut became a natural base for spies and newsmen to monitor other Arab countries, oil agreements, the Arab-Israeli conflict and the manoeuvres of the superpowers. Its very make-up facilitated the gathering and transmission of information of all kinds.

For spies, it was Switzerland, Tangiers and Casablanca all rolled into one: a sophisticated, extremely pleasant, neutral country complete with seedy fleshpots full of whores, pimps, smugglers, drug dealers and mercenary assassins. I have known spies to pose as banker, foreign correspondent, barman, professor, business consultant, salesmen of various types, dancer, waiter, public relations man, oil man and archaeologist. With the Middle East in constant turmoil, Beirut was a veritable revolving door for information.

If spies found fertile ground there, Beirut was an even more accommodating base for foreign correspondents, with its welcoming Lebanese culture and every conceivable practical facility for news-gathering. Unlike other Middle Eastern cities, Beirut suffered no censorship, it boasted comparatively good communication facilities and Middle East Airlines provided regular, scheduled flights to all parts of the Arab world. Beirut had more newspapers than London and more news bulletins than Paris, no currency exchange restrictions and a sophisticated local press corps ready to help outsiders. In the words of the former correspondent for London's *Daily Mail*, Anthony Cave Brown: 'It was an amazing listening post, everything and everyone passed through it.'

All were drawn to Beirut – from the politicians of neighbouring countries to businessmen of every stripe – by the same essential elements. No other city of the region could offer its availability of multi-lingual secretarial and managerial talent or ultra-modern office buildings. In Beirut, the dress and behaviour of females was not encumbered by either custom or religion, and a wife could be left alone at home during her husband's business travels. Most of all, Beirut was neutral territory, a place where Arabs' national jealousies were overcome: a Saudi would object to having his regional headquarters in Kuwait, or an Iraqi in Saudi Arabia, but Beirut was acceptable to all.

Even as Beirut was the centre of the Middle East, so the undisputed centre of Beirut was the St George Hotel, and the heart of the hotel, the single spot where the more important congregated to know, help, promote, compete with, undermine and even destroy each other, was the bar.

The bar's unique position was attained by dint of circumstance and hard work. Along with the Normandy and the Royal Hotels, the St George had been one of Beirut's leading hotels ever since its construction by a French company in the thirties for the use of French colonial officers. As such, it was a natural beneficiary of the good fortune which enveloped all Beirut from the early fifties onward. But its exceptional natural location and superior quality of service on all levels enabled the St George to outdistance its competitors and preserve its leading position.

The five-storey concrete-block building stands on a small piece of land reclaimed from the Mediterranean and sur-rounded by water on three sides. Sited in the heart of Beirut, it faces the near-perfect Bay of Jounieh and, across this, the mountains which rush up from the sea to tease the beautifully blue sky with their snow-capped tops, their sides dotted from bottom to top with idyllic villages set amid pine forests and citrus groves. Each floor of the building is girdled by a balcony so sub-divided as to provide each room with its own little patio. A semi-circular ground-floor terrace extended in a south-easterly direction, affording a full view of the bay and the mountains.

On rare days in early spring or autumn, you could sit on the terrace for a noonday drink and watch people snow- and water-skiing within a single line of vision. At night, the village lights rose with the mountains until they became difficult to distinguish from the stars. No other place in Beirut or, to my knowledge, in the world, could duplicate its beauty of location.

As if this mesmerizing view was not enough, the St George Hotel was made all the more inviting by its human fac-tor. Almost every participant in the affairs of the hotel, right down to the most humble employee, was moved by something beyond mere duty. Myrna Bustani saw her part-ownership as the equivalent of a national trust. When Jean Bertolet was general manager, he rose early to buy fresh-caught fish and personally inspected the meat flown in every day from the Boucherie Meurbouf in Paris. The concierge, Mansour Breidy, would not tolerate the slightest speck of dust on any of his bellhops' uniforms; Mohammad Mseitif, the doorman, demanded that taxi drivers servicing the hotel keep their cars clean; bar manager Ali Bitar had each and every bottle dusted daily; and bartender Abu Khalil grew his own peppers for use in mixing Bloody Marys. Everyone, from the owner to the shoe-shine man, felt compelled to give the world their very best.

The raw statistics of the place evoke little of its atmosphere. The hotel's two revolving doors concealed a whole world inside: one hundred and ten rooms and suites, eight shops, a spacious lobby which could seat sixty people, a large conference and party saloon, a bar, grill room and terrace. Despite the old-fashioned elegance of its interiors, the hotel's true distinction lay in the number of employees – two hundred and eighty five in all. With such a large and so devoted a staff, it is easy to see how the St George maintained its reputation for exceptional service, which was excellent even by the most exacting of international standards.

The bar embraced an inner bar-room with a small annexe reserved for private parties, the grill room and the terrace. The wood-panelled bar-room could seat forty-six people, either at the nine round, glass-topped tables with their classic leather chairs, or on regular bar stools facing the fifteen-foot wooden bar. The bar-room opened directly on to the terrace, which was filled with potted plants and enough metal tables and chairs to seat another seventy people and which shared the south-eastern corner of the hotel with the grill room, which could seat a further fifty people. A generous ratio of twenty-two on-duty staff were assigned to serve the bar's potential one hundred and sixty-six customers.

The outstanding service provided by the hotel and in the bar surpassed all reasonable expectation. John Chancellor of the US National Broadcasting Company (NBC) is still rightly impressed by the quality of the services offered: 'They kept my mail, hired my cars, sent my telegrams and nodded discreetly to direct me towards important people. Go away for a few weeks and everything was arranged when you got back. Curfew passes, visas, you name it.' *Time* correspondent Gavin Scott remembers that the press corps received and sent its mail via the concierge's desk. American banker Paul Parker has described the grill room as one of 'the best restaurants in the world'. Anthony Cavendish, former agent of MI6, the espionage department of British Military Intelligence, recalls that 'everything was perfect after the first visit – they got to know your likes and dislikes and remembered them'. Bill MacLaughlin of the US Columbia Broadcasting System (CBS) tells how head barman Ali Bitar advised him exactly whom to bribe at the PTT in order to arrange the installation of a telex machine within three days – a happy end to an agonizing four months of trying conventional European means. St John Philby, the Orientalist, and his son, Kim, both received the news of the deaths of their respective first wives at the St George, in both cases via cables transmitted to the St George because their exact whereabouts in Lebanon were unknown.

The important people drawn to the bar endowed it with its special character; the clientele became part of the attraction. The fictional Rick's of the film *Casablanca* seems but a pale shadow of the authentic St George Hotel bar.

None of the *Casablanca* spies who frequented Rick's compares with Kim Philby, a bar regular for five years and one of the biggest spies of all time. There was no *Casablanca* character so lethal or twisted as the CIA agent James Russell Barracks, another bar regular. The overall importance and immediate consequence of politics discussed and acted upon in the bar leave political happenings at Rick's way behind. The Rick-Elsa-Laslow romantic triangle falls short of the real-life drama of Kim Philby winning Eleanor Philby from her previous husband, *New York Times* correspondent Sam Pope Brewer. Information pedlars to be found in the bar made Peter Lorre seem an also-ran dealing only in small-time stuff.

Political conspiracies hatched in the corners of the bar have altered the map of the Middle East and changed the course of global power politics. Hundred-million-dollar business deals were struck at its glass-topped tables. Its wood-panelled walls witnessed campaigns of disinformation and news manipulation with far-reaching consequences to journalism and democratic society.

In writing a book about the St George Hotel bar, I pay humble tribute to its truth-is-stranger-than-fiction legend. I do believe that happenings in that little place have in all likelihood affected all our lives, however indirectly. But this is intended to be an entertaining look backward to the place where my misspent youth was misspent. Step aside Mr Rick, here come the real players.

'You don't invent or plan places like the bar – they just happen.'

Ali Bitar, head barman

'A place like it – no. There was no place like it; there is no place like it.'

Jean Bertolet, general manager, St George Hotel

'They had the location. They had good food. They had an excellent concierge. They had an exceptional head barman. That's what made the place.'

Sheikh Najib Allumedine, former chairman, Middle East Airlines

2

A DAY IN THE LIFE
OF THE
ST GEORGE HOTEL BAR

For well over twenty years, from the early fifties until 1975, those who followed developments in the Middle East were wont to utter the key phrase, 'lets go to the bar and find out'. An ordinary day at the bar in the fifties might reveal a plot to assassinate an Arab leader, while the sixties was a period of financial manipulations involving hundreds of millions of dollars and the early seventies were devoted to solving Lebanon's seemingly insoluble problems. Only by living through a typical day at the St George Hotel bar is it possible to appreciate its pivotal rôle in the events of the region and of the world. I am opting for a day in the autumn of 1959 as a case in point, a day when I was there, an eye-witness to most occurrences, a party to some and very much an impressionable young man of twenty-four energetically capable of noticing most happenings though, unlike now, not capable of digesting the meaning of more than a few.

The first man to arrive at the bar was Sam Pope Brewer, chief Middle East correspondent of the *New York Times*. Sam, then fifty-five, was a large man of about six feet three inches who always dressed in a sober grey suit and waistcoat. He stopped at the concierge's desk to collect his mail and cablegrams, neatly folded them inside the newspapers and magazines he was carrying, rolled the whole lot up and placed the bundle firmly under his left arm before marching towards the bar with long deliberate steps, as if he were walking through an official function. This was between ten-thirty and ten-forty-five in the morning.

That day, like many others, Brewer's regular routine was

witnessed by the group of young reporters – including Larry Collins of United Press International (UPI), Dick Kallsen of CBS, Richard Beeston of the now-defunct *London News Chronicle*, Tom Streithorst of NBC and me, representing Radio Free Europe (RFE) – who normally gathered at that hour in the long hotel lobby opposite the concierge's desk to exchange views about current events and a possible story for the day. When Sam Brewer passed through, totally oblivious to our presence, someone's irreverent comment about the Ten A.M. Club triggered a round of giggles and sharp, short comments about the aptly named unofficial body and its members. Nobody can recall why we dubbed it the Ten A.M. Club, since its members came in closer to eleven.

Despite our irreverent comments about Brewer, we all liked him, appreciated his gentlemanly Southern manners and admired his record as a star foreign correspondent during the Spanish Civil War, the Second World War and the 1948 Arab-Israeli War. And we were fully sympathetic with the personal unhappiness which drove him to heavy drinking: Eleanor, his wife of ten years, had left him to marry Kim Philby, later exposed as one of the super-spies of the century. Our irreverence did not extend to discussing this matter openly.

With us in the lobby at that hour were various other groups who also gathered in clusters around their own tables every day. There was a cluster of Their Excellencies, the well-healed Lebanese who met regularly to slurp endless cups of Turkish coffee and exchange views and gossip about their country's position in the world. These representatives of Lebanon's business and political élite related more to the international world of the hotel than to the problems threatening the future of their own country. Near them sat a group of political refugees from neighbouring Arab countries with tired voices and tired faces and no light in their eyes, discussing the dictatorial régimes governing their homelands and expressing their anxieties by the speed with which they clicked their worry beads. A third table had two American businessmen in short sleeves and crew-cuts unfolding large, cumbersome blueprints and explaining them to an Arab from an oil-rich state. One group which never clustered in the lobby was the spies. They only used the bar.

According to Ali Bitar, who managed the St George Hotel bar for sixteen years, Sam Pope Brewer had very little to say for himself at that hour of the morning. He would stand at the bar, grunt a yes in response to 'The usual, Mr Brewer?' and then read his newspapers and correspondence while slowly sipping his Gibson (a dry martini cocktail with an onion instead of an olive or lemon peel) and waiting for 'the co-chairman of the Ten A.M. Club', Wilbur Crane (Bill) Eveland, a known CIA operative who usually arrived ten to fifteen minutes after Sam in a black, chauffeur-driven limousine of the type usually reserved for diplomats. (Eveland eventually recorded his spying exploits in a book, *Ropes of Sand*.)

Bill Eveland was younger and slimmer than Sam, just as tall, but lacking Sam's courtly, aristocratic demeanour. He unfailingly waved a friendly hello to us as he sped toward the bar to join his friend, and that day was no exception. As we returned Bill's greeting, we exchanged the usual furtive smiles which implicitly acknowledged Sam's sad reliance on Bill for what he wrote. No longer a great foreign correspondent, Sam had been reduced to a has-been mouthpiece for the CIA.

Sam and Bill held their daily secret conversations as the staff prepared for the day. Every bottle, chair and ashtray was set in place: small plates were filled with nuts, olives and potato crisps, ready to serve with the drinks. The glass tops of the round tables were polished to a high shine, the tools to mix drinks were symmetrically arranged atop the long wooden bar for maximum accessibility and the door to the terrace was swung wide open to admit fresh air and sun. Meanwhile, the *New York Times* and the CIA huddled over Gibsons and whisky-and-soda to organize what the world was going to hear the following day, a doctored version of the US government's point of view. In the words of NBC's young and idealistic Streithorst, 'a sad day for journalism'.

At about noon, well after our contemporaries had departed

with the very energetic Larry Collins in the lead, Streithorst and I decided to have a rare drink at the bar. Noon was the time when most of the bar regulars arrived. Our modest salaries and expense accounts only allowed the occasional visit.

Joseph Bedarian, then head barman, was in his usual place behind the bar, impeccably attired in a white jacket and black trousers, with his eyes everywhere. Ali Bitar, the head waiter who later replaced Joseph, was at the door greeting arrivals and helping them to their tables as the cashier, the Armenian bartender and two waiters saw to their duties. Streithorst and I took a table at the back of the room – facing the bar, and the backs of Sam and Bill, and in full view of incoming traffic – and ordered two relatively inexpensive beers.

The most punctual noon-time arrivals were John Mecklin and my father, Abu Saïd, both of *Time* magazine. They arrived a minute or two after we did, exchanged a perfunctory greeting with Sam and Bill and waved hello to us while sitting down to their scotches and water at Abu Saïd's regular table, the only one in the bar with a view both of arrivals and of everyone in the place.

Mecklin, thin, tall, crew-cut, and handsome, with an ever-present look of a naughty boy, was Sam's chief rival among the foreign correspondents; his reporting had taken strong exception to US foreign policy in the Middle East, particularly its commitment to traditional rulers such as Hussein of Jordan and Saud of Saudi Arabia. Instead, he championed Nasser of Egypt, an extremely popular leader who was, according to the US and Brewer, pro-Russian. Mecklin dismissed Nasser's flirtation with Russia as an act of convenience which lacked ideological kinship. To him, the Arabs were not ready for the rigidness of communist ideology and he thought Nasser's dream of uniting all Arabs in one big country, instead of a band of weak ones, worthy of consideration, perhaps even support.

Streithorst and I toed the Mecklin line, as did most other correspondents, but there were other powerful voices backing Sam's attitude, notably James Wallace of the US *Wall Street*

Journal. Sam considered the Arabs to be decades removed from effective self-rule, and his writing betrayed a boredom with the Middle East and with the world in general. Mecklin, on the other hand, a graduate of Dartmouth College, where his father had taught, was idealistic and energetic, and his reporting investigative in nature, entertaining an appealing populist streak and a concern for the Arab of the mosque and the *souk*. He was a very good writer.

So the St George Hotel bar, where Sam got his CIA information from Bill Eveland and where Mecklin debriefed his sources, also was the battleground for their sharp rivalry, which, unhappily, descended to a personal level. Brewer's comments about Mecklin reflected a distinct impatience with a brash young man (Mecklin was thirty-seven): 'basically superficial, more interested in womanizing than in real news'. Mecklin hit back in an outspoken way, bitterly accusing Sam of laziness and, on account of his dependence on Eveland, betrayal of the trust placed in him by the *New York Times*, and of the unsuspecting public who believed in the rôle of the foreign correspondent as an independent observer and in the impartiality of the *Times*.

The conflict which arose from the two men's differing characters and temperaments was exacerbated by the worldwide competition between their respective news organizations. Locally, *Time* had successfully poached my father, Abu Saïd, from the *New York Times* with the lure of a higher salary.

Characteristically, Abu Saïd's first act after ordering a drink was to ask the head waiter, Ali Bitar, whether anyone besides the people present had come in. Ali, speaking in Arabic, always answered in a code of flowery Arabic description rather than the proper names known to all. 'Assistant to the little king' meant Radi Abdallah, military aide-de-camp to King Hussein; 'the activist from your country' meant Shafiq El Hout of the Palestine Liberation Organization (PLO); and 'the spokesman for the big man' meant Mohammed Hasanein Heikal, editor-in-chief of the Egyptian daily, *Al Ahram*, and Nasser's right-hand man.

That day, however, Ali had nothing to report. That day only Al Shabab, the young ones, Streithorst and I were in.

Abu Saïd then spoke briefly with members of the bar staff as he always did. They were his friends, the people who kept him informed of who saw whom, what they drank and ate and, when possible, what they said. His Arabness and meticulous care in never compromising them as sources of information endeared him to them, but it was his genuine friendliness at all times, even when in the company of the high and mighty, which made him special. He respected and addressed their individual concerns, be it their children's schooling or their political affiliations. And they put Abu Saïd before the offers of money for information which they received almost daily.

While Abu Saïd carried on with his daily ritual, Kim Philby, still unexposed, ostensibly a correspondent for *The Economist* and the *Observer*, arrived at his usual time of one p.m., accompanied by Ralph Izzard of the *Daily Mail*. Kim's stocky figure contrasted with Ralph's slim six-foot five-inch frame, but both wore corduroy trousers and sports jackets. Kim characteristically pushed back his boyish shock of hair and stammered a good morning to his wife's ex-husband, Sam Brewer, sending out a signal that he had been drinking, no doubt observing his normal routine of an eleven a.m. stop at the Normandy Hotel followed by a leisurely walk to the St George, a mere kilometre away. Kim and Ralph occupied a front-row table next to Mecklin and Abu Saïd, behind Sam and Bill. Kim had his usual gin and tonic, while Ralph settled for a whisky and water; their dress, manner of ordering drinks and way of eating the appetizers attested to their unmistakable Englishness. Noticing Kim's condition, Streithorst and I again resorted to an old bar cliché and spoke of Kim as 'neither observing nor economizing'.

Soon the bar filled up. Emir Majid Arslan, a short, paunchy man with a handlebar moustache and fez, arrived alone and sat near Streithorst and myself on a chair especially raised to make him look taller. A Lebanese Druze leader and six times Minister of Defence, this colourful, extremely polite man spoke in a thin voice which contrasted with his awesome demeanour. He was followed by Jamil Pasha Abdel Wahab, who had been Minister of Education under the Iraqi monarchist régime which was toppled in 1958 and who in 1959 was an exile constantly conspiring to restore the throne. Then John Bouchow of Morgan Guaranty Trust Co. walked in with Joseph Ellender, a vice president of government relations with Aramco, the consortium of oil companies with a monopoly in Saudi Arabia. The banker looked like a transplant from Wall Street, while the oil man seemed at ease with his surroundings and his manner of walking and talking made his presence in the bar more natural than that of his banker friend.

The day-time party was in full swing. Iraqi monarchist Jamil Pasha joined Mecklin and Abu Saïd, who quizzed him about conditions in his country under dictator Abdel Karim Kassem, trying to confirm reports that Kassem was arming the communist-led People's Militia, a move which could have had far-reaching consequences in terms of Russian penetration of the Middle East. Like exiles everywhere, Jamil Pasha was anxious to talk, but had nothing new to tell.

Amazingly, the Englishmen Philby and Izzard were discussing their children. Ralph Izzard told me recently that he and Kim Philby always discussed politics and news stories at the Normandy earlier in the day and made a point of limiting themselves to everyday conversation at the St George Hotel bar because they rightly assumed that people were listening to them. Soon they were joined by Kim's wife, Eleanor, Sam's former wife. She, too, had obviously been drinking and she greeted Eveland and her ex-husband, Sam Brewer, as darlings in a manner which betrayed her Washington state background. Eleanor was tall, a little loud and her once-pretty face showed clear signs of heavy drinking, which her sunglasses always confirmed.

John Fistere, a handsome, grey-haired American with Eastern establishment manners doing public relations for King Hussein of Jordan, came to the bar with a moustached little

Arab named Amin Hafez Bazian, owner of Amman's best-known flower shop, but, more important and remarkable, a close friend and confidant of Haza Pasha Al Majali, the prime minister of Jordan. Fistere and Bazian were important to each other; the first had the ear of the king and the second the ear of the prime minister.

His Excellency Emir Majid Arslan, the portly local politician, was soon joined by His Excellency Raymond Edde, a Lebanese member of parliament and former cabinet member with presidential ambitions. Jamil Pasha left Mecklin and Abu Saïd after delivering his regular sermon in praise of the monarchy to sit in a far corner exchanging whispers with a mysterious Iraqi who was clicking his worry beads nervously. Finally, James Russell Barracks, tall, bespectacled and Brooks-Brothers-attired, walked in and shook the hands of no less than seven people, pumping Kim Philby's extra hard. He sat alone at a table after motioning me to join him when I was free.

I joined Barracks a little after two in the afternoon, when Tom Streithorst left to go home. That day Barracks' greeting to me was overdone, even by his own showy standards, and he was full of unusual interest in my work and well-being.

Banker Bouchow, unusually glum after an unsatisfactory conversation in which Ellender stubbornly refused to divulge Aramco's estimate for Saudi Arabia's oil income in the next three years, joined Mecklin and Abu Saïd. According to my father, Bouchow, whom he had met two or three times before, was preoccupied with most unusual problems, telling Mecklin and my father that Morgan Guaranty, his employer, had information to the effect that the religious leaders in Saudi Arabia were considering forcing the spendthrift King Saud to step down in favour of his conservative brother, Prince Faisal. Could the *Time* magazine team check it out? In view of Saudi Arabia's huge deposits with Morgan Guaranty, Bouchow's concern to verify the story is easy to understand. Mecklin and Abu Saïd had known that all was not well in Saudi Arabia, but had no idea that such a major, far-reaching move was in the offing. Bouchow knew they had extensive contacts throughout the Middle East and was counting on their help to verify his story in return for his tip-off about it.

Only a few yards away, Lebanese presidential hopeful Raymond Edde was trying to persuade fellow politician Emir Majid to join him in forming a parliamentary opposition block to topple the Lebanese Cabinet. Theirs was a most uneasy discussion. The suave, worldly, French-educated Edde was having a difficult time communicating his doubts about the then government to the very tribal Druze chief. It was as if the two Lebanese politicians spoke different languages, something we have by now come to expect from Lebanese politicians.

Barracks' conversation with me did not transcend social banality until the Kim Philby group had left. He then asked me whether Kim came to the bar on a regular basis, something he already knew, and he inquired if Kim spent an inordinate amount of time talking to any of the bar waiters. When I shrugged my shoulders, Barracks asked me to have lunch with him at Loculus Restaurant the following day, making it very plain that Kim Philby was on his mind.

The bead-clicking Iraqi huddled in the corner with Jamil Pasha was Issa Selim Al Zeiback, later a close friend of mine. His whispers were justified, for he was telling his fellow countryman of a plot to assassinate the Iraqi dictator Kassem scheduled to be carried out within a few days. Zeiback's information came from his own son Selim, one of the would-be assassins. While favouring Kassem's elimination, Jamil Pasha cautioned against the likely dire consequences of such an attempt, which might allow the communists to assume direct rule, particularly since the would-be assassins had no plan for a follow-up to assume control themselves – nor, for that matter, could his people, the royalists, undertake such a move.

By comparison, Fistere's conversation with Bazian was a down-to-earth discussion of the long-term problem of corruption. Bazian complained that certain members of the Jordanian royal family, the king's relations, were undermining his friend the prime minister through involvement in smuggling and bribery, a refrain the cagey Fistere deflected by saying only that no one dared speak to His Majesty about his relations.

By three-thirty the bar was empty except for two groups: four Lebanese sitting at the bar (lawyer George Bueiz, journalist Marc Riashi, a government employee and an unknown) plus a table of four Americans planning a sales convention for Westinghouse. Besides the people mentioned by name, about fifteen others had come and gone; in all, about forty people visited the bar at noon, considerably fewer than usual, though the momentous subjects of conversation were typical.

In the late afternoon Joseph Bedarian, the head barman, went home for his siesta, leaving everything in the capable hands of his head waiter and deputy Ali Bitar. Ali, who had a keen eye for the unusual, had noted Bouchow's table-hopping and uncharacteristic edginess, Barracks' over-friendliness towards me, as well as the rare light of hope which shone in the eyes of the two Iraqi exiles. But he spent little time speculating on their portent. He took them in his stride.

That day my schedule called for me to return to the bar at six p.m. to discuss the family with my father, Abu Saïd. I had assumed, wrongly, that the bar would be empty of journalists, politicians, businessmen and spies, and that my father and I would relax over a drink and talk about my brothers' performance at their universities and other personal concerns. Arriving on time, I was surprised to find him already there with Mecklin engaged in friendly conversation with a smaller, darker version of Lenin – bald pate, goatee, rumpled brown suit, et al. They motioned me to join them to meet Farhan Al Gahtani, then excused themselves to continue interviewing him for what Mecklin called 'not a RFE type of story'.

Indeed it wasn't. Farhan represented the vanguard of a type which became better known in the early seventies: the semi-literate peninsula Arab who struck it rich in the oil-induced construction boom. The now-familiar story had all the necessary ingredients: growing up in a tent, wandering into the Aramco compound barefoot, learning how to read and write English in an Aramco night school (but without ever becoming literate in Arabic), parleying a job as a truck driver into an extremely lucrative contracting business which had already yielded him millions of dollars. Farhan had a most appealing twinkle in his eyes, considerable native intelligence, plus an appreciation of the benefits of a story about him in the business section of *Time* magazine.

The conversation with Farhan, respectfully addressed as sheikh by an admiring Mecklin, lasted an hour, until seven p.m., and was as engrossing to me as to the interviewer. This fascinating preview of things to come made us oblivious to the arrival of about twenty people: tourists and monied Lebanese out for a night on the town, as well as a minor Lebanese excellency who stood at the bar laughing and grunting, smugly and crudely making fun of everyone in the place, confirming the suspicion that he was a secret police plant.

Shafiq El Hout, the handsome, dapper, PLO-type then-editor of *Al Hawadess Weekly* and leading authority on socialism in the Middle East, was sitting with his girlfriend on the terrace. Kheiry Hammad, ostensibly a correspondent for Continentale, an Italian news agency specializing in reporting communist activities, but in reality a top intelligence agent of Nasser's United Arab Republic (UAR), the short-lived union of Egypt and Syria, had deposited his grossly fat figure on a stool in front of us. John Mecom, Sr, the unmistakable picture of a Texas oil baron, was seated in a far corner surrounded by a Texan court, all attired in ten-gallon hats and boots and all bursting with happy loud talk. At another table there lurked the lonely figure of Bouchow, the unhappy banker. Others unknown to me were scattered around the place.

Farhan Al Gahtani lost his argument with Mecklin over who should settle the bill and, not to be out-done, promptly extended an invitation for the three of us to join him later that evening at Al Casbah Night Club, where the famous belly dancer Fadya Ibrahim was performing. The invitation was accepted, deadlines and news stories permitting.

As Farhan left, singing the praises of his favourite belly dancer, an anxious Mecklin leaned over and told me the question posed by Bouchow earlier in the day: whether a Saudi palace coup was in the making. As luck would have it, I expected to see Abdallah Al Tariki, then Saudi Minister of Petroleum and Mineral Resources, in the bar that evening. I had established a friendly enough relationship with Tariki to permit me to ask him the question, off the record. Tariki's answer, Mecklin and I agreed, would tell us whether the story was worth pursuing. We would discuss this at the Casbah, after I had seen Tariki.

Mecklin joined Bouchow just as Akef Pasha Al Fayez entered with two companions. Akef Pasha and my father embraced, Arab-style, visibly pleased to see each other, and then he and I embraced. There was an expectant stir from the Texas camp, but Akef Pasha Al Fayez, never a man to be rushed, told my father he wished to see him alone, at a table in the corner where Ali stood ready to seat him after giving him a genuinely warm handshake. The noticeable commotion within Mecom's group subsided after Al Fayez transmitted a message through Ali that he would join them in ten minutes.

In the meantime, Kheiry Hammad and I joined the PLO's Shafiq El Hout and his friend to discuss everyday happenings in the Middle East. Ali, who had his own way of showing affection, put a full complement of appetizers on our table, double the usual portions of potato crisps, pistachios and peanuts. A devout Moslem and ardent Arab Nationalist, Ali liked Shafiq, Kheiry and myself, always treating us in a special way.

Ali then attended to two new arrivals, Afif Al Tibi and Hanna Ghossun, the editors, respectively, of Arabic-language dailies *Al Youm* and *Al Diar*. The charming, famous duo ordered drinks while quizzing Ali about the Raymond Edde meeting earlier in the day with Emir Majid Arslan. Ali would only verify that the two had met, but denied any knowledge of the conversation between the two Lebanese politicians. Ghossun now reflects that he liked Ali 'because he never said anything, an extremely discreet man'. Ghossun and

Tibi spent close to two hours discussing the implications for internal Lebanese politics of an Edde-Arslan alliance.

A mere two tables away Abu Saïd was trying to help Akef Pasha Al Fayez, the handsome sheikh of sheikhs of Bani Sakr, Jordan's biggest tribe, and many times minister and deputy prime minister. Status mattered less to Abu Saïd than Al Fayez's position as an honoured personal friend of long standing, a true pre-oil sheikh with inherent bedouin decency and grace. Al Fayez hoped to check the credentials of Texas oil man Mecom, who had solicited his help in securing a concession to explore for oil in Jordan. Abu Saïd could only promise to seek information from Bouchow, the representative of 'the bankers' bankers'.

As Al Fayez joined the most welcoming Texan group, Abu Saïd sat with Mecklin and Bouchow, and I left El Hout and Hammad to join oil minister Abdallah Al Tariki, who had come in, greeted Ali quietly and sat in a secluded corner all by himself.

Al Tariki, a Texas-educated oil engineer and, with Perez of Venezuela, co-founder of the Organization of Petroleum-Exporting Countries (OPEC), looked very tired. A shortish round man with a dark complexion, he was a workaholic, a soft-spoken, deliberate man of unmistakable style and authority who publicly drank Perrier water out of deference to Saudi religious laws. His greeting was subdued, but his mere presence there told of his exceptional generosity and far-sightedness, which included genuine interest in and concern for the younger generation, myself included. He had come especially to see me and I took pleasure in his elegant company.

Had I known of Al Fayez's inquiry about Mecom, Al Tariki would have been the best man to ask, but I was occupied with the royal family squabble in Saudi Arabia and its potential consequences. When I broached the question, and after some prodding, Al Tariki made a very telling statement which said all and nothing at all. Sighing deeply, he very coldly asked, 'What do you think happens when the second in command in a country is more intelligent and able than the top man?'

Then he changed subjects and began to quiz me about my latest dispatches to Radio Free Europe, particularly how I came to select the specific subject matter for my weekly report. My forty-five-minute meeting with Tariki was as edifying as usual.

I returned to Hammad and El Hout full of praise for Tariki's decency and intelligence. Not only did they agree, but El Hout reflected prophetically that 'They [the House of Saud] will get rid of him. There is no room for able counsellors in their plans.' Serious discussion didn't follow; instead El Hout and I proceeded to improvise a joke reflecting our disdain for the House of Saud which I remember to this day. It went like this:

The military aide-de-camp to the king of Saudi Arabia enters the latter's office, salutes grimly and asks for permission to speak, which is granted.

'Your Majesty, the Israelis have an atomic bomb!'

'Is that important, son?' asks the king.

'Extremely important, Majesty. We, too, must have one.'

'Then by all means buy one, get money from the treasury and buy one.'

Then, as His Majesty's satisfied aide turns to leave, the king decides to add a proviso to his purchase order: 'Son, please make sure the model you buy is air-conditioned.'

Hammad bounced with happy laughter, but El Hout's girlfriend, who appreciated the joke, cautioned us against telling it to anyone. Naturally, I vowed to tell it to Tariki – which I never did. Hammad, anxious to avoid an argument, decided to tell a joke of his own, but looked around first to ensure that no outsiders were listening. The joke told how an American businessman takes a shine to the Lebanese newspaper boy who sells him his daily *International Herald Tribune* and decides to teach the boy how to count in English. Each day the businessman asked his protégé a counting question and supplied the answer. On the fifth day, he had no sooner asked the boy what two and two made, than he was shocked into remembering that he was in Lebanon when the boy stared him in the eye and said: 'Buying or selling?' Again, we roared with laughter.

It was nearing nine-thirty p.m. and the bar was once again emptying. Ghossun and Tibi left still deep in animated conversation, Al Fayez departed after telling Mecom that he 'would look into things', Mecklin and Abu Saïd told Bouchow they were expecting an answer soon, Hammad and El Hout went in different directions and even non-regulars who were there to have a drink in the famous place were deciding that the day was done and it was time to move on. I left to go home for a two-hour nap in preparation for a long evening with Farhan Al Gahtani; the show at the Casbah would not start until midnight.

Looking back on that day, I scold myself for the vanity of my youth, for my failure to inquire about the visitors I didn't know, some probably with stories as exciting as those of the regulars. In the words of Ali Bitar, 'We didn't appreciate what was a bar stool or a table away – let's face it, we were in one of the most exciting places on earth.'

Every single conversation that day in the bar pointed to much larger movements in the Middle East which bespoke a whole region undergoing unsettled transition fraught with turmoil and instability. Placed in their proper context, these conversations were indicators of the momentous events which shaped and continue to form the Middle East as we know it today.

The meeting between Jamil Pasha and Issa Al Zeiback was to discuss the fate of their country, Iraq, then as now of immense geopolitical importance to the balance of power in the Middle East. Both Jamil Pasha and Al Zeiback had a common enemy in the country's then dictator Abdul Karim Kassem and both were committed to his overthrow, but the two could not agree on what type of régime should replace his Russian-leaning populist government. Jamil Pasha favoured the restoration of a monarchist system under King Hussein of Jordan, the cousin of the country's last monarch, while Al Zeiback wanted to integrate Iraq into Nasser's Arab Unity schemes by making it part of the UAR.

As it turned out, the entire Middle East reeled under the effects of an assassination attempt which left Kassem severely wounded and slightly demented. The lack of organized follow-up to take control of the government in the wake of the attempt limited its consequences. Al Zeiback's son was indeed one of the three assassins (as was Saddam Hussein, Iraq's current president); he was captured and later died under torture. Iraq's problems continue to plague the region and there is no permanence to its present government.

Bouchow's scuttle-butt proved correct. Prince Faisal of Saudi Arabia replaced his brother King Saud, with far-reaching results, not only for Morgan Guaranty Trust Co., but for the political texture of the Arab World. Faisal's conservatism provided the bulwark against which Nasser's ambitions foundered; he supported the Yemenis against Nasser's plans to annex their country, in the process dragging Nasser into a war he couldn't afford, one which overtaxed the Egyptian budget and demoralized Egypt's army – in a way, the beginning of the end for Nasser.

Sadly, El Hout's prediction of Tariki's fate came true. His brand of oil nationalism ran foul of the Saudi royal family's inherent conservatism and he was dismissed to live in exile. To this day, he acts as an oil consultant to Colonel Gadafi of Libya and the Algerian government. The Saudi royal family, who continue to view their country as a private piece of real estate, eventually meted out the same treatment to Tariki's successor, the famous, but less talented Sheikh Zaki Yamani.

Farhan Al Gahtani's case perfectly illustrates an all-too-frequent tragedy in the fast-changing Middle East. After amassing a fortune of about twenty million dollars, his weakness for pretty girls and the limelight came ahead of work and he fell prey to Lebanese wheeler-dealers. He went broke and beat a retreat into the desert, a broken man with stories of what was and what might have been. His type are a whole social class.

El Hout is part of the PLO's national command, one of its leading international spokesmen. He betrays clear signs of cynicism and his initial revolutionary élan has been replaced by a forced submission to the policies of accommodation. These days, the king of Saudi Arabia does not order air-conditioned atomic bombs, but is a sponsor of the PLO; his ignorance, profligate ways, intolerance of intelligence and womanizing are things to be overlooked.

Fistere maintained and expanded his position with King Hussein over a period of twenty years. A former Office of Strategic Services (OSS) officer whose demeanour and behaviour were appropriate to Madison Avenue, he exhibited no real understanding of the Middle East and often led Hussein into troublesome, uncharted territory through sheer, pretentious ignorance. Fistere is now known to have been a CIA agent. Certainly his behaviour, more accurately misbehaviour, pushed King Hussein away from his people and towards total reliance on a short-sighted US foreign policy inimical to them.

The behaviour of leading CIA agent James Russell Barracks that day and his evident desire to monitor Philby have ominous implications. Surely this was an early sign of the budding feud between the CIA and the British Intelligence establishment, the one which gained impetus with Philby's eventual defection. True, Barracks was slimey, almost vulgar, and his behaviour bordered on the naive, but he could not have initiated a Philby watch and paid for it without higher approval.

No less significant was the manipulation of Brewer by the CIA and its deliberate use of the *New York Times* to advance its point of view. This clear attempt to turn one man's personal misfortune to use was made all the more unpalatable by the reputation Brewer had once enjoyed, as well as by the influence of the *New York Times* – indeed 'a sad day for journalism'.

This period marked the beginning of American banks' concern with political developments as a determining factor in their Middle East fortunes; dozens of banks were to realize this in the future. Men like Mecom were flooding into the Middle East in huge do-or-die efforts (Mecom's failed), some of which yielded instant fortunes in the Gulf and Libya.

Even the intricacy and dichotomy of Lebanese politics made an appearance that day. Amid Nasser's attempts to subvert the country, the West's desire to control it and Russia's desire to use it as a base for regional penetration, the super-suave Edde attempted to ally himself across a huge divide with the totally tribal Arslan, while the Lebanese press was there in friendly alliance checking on their country's changing fortunes – totally dismissive of Hout and Hammad, Palestinians whose presence in Lebanon eventually contributed to that nation's disintegration.

What was lacking that day was clear evidence of the inherent savagery of the intelligence business, day-to-day nastiness among the press corps and seriously dirty business dealings. Philby, Eveland, Barracks, Fistere, Hammad, Ellender of Aramco, possibly two journalists and the unpleasant Lebanese grunter were all spies. Mecklin, Brewer, Streithorst, Beeston, Izzard, Collins, Tibi, Ghossun and El Hout were competing journalists. Bouchow was a banker and, beyond his intelligence work, Ellender represented a major oil company. We shall hear more about their behaviour towards each other and the rest of the world later.

'It was the ambiance of suggestive disinformation which made visits [to the bar] essential . . . rumours, whiffs of fact and of course self-serving claims . . . notable visitors everywhere.'

Gavin Scott, *Time* magazine correspondent

'Radi . . . go to the St George bar and find out if the rumour of a plot against us is true. Someone there will know.'

King Hussein of Jordan to his military aide-de-camp

'A large number of newspaper correspondents flocked to the city, making the St George Hotel their headquarters.'

Archie Roosevelt, CIA station chief

3

THE FIRST DRAFT OF HISTORY – ST GEORGE HOTEL BAR VERSION

Myrna Bustani has applied her simple, attractive, un-Lebanese and undramatic way of reducing things to essentials to the use of the bar by journalists: 'If you wanted to know the news before it appeared in the media, then you went to the bar. Both the people who made the news and the people who reported it gathered there.'

Our concern in this chapter is the group of journalists who used the bar to prepare their first draft of history, a group we shall refer to as the bar press and which included a large percentage of the foreign journalists who covered the Middle East and many important local journalists. There were Lebanese and, particularly after the advent of broadcast journalism, Americans, but also British, French, Russian, Canadian, Italian, Japanese, Egyptian, Scandinavian and others – journalists of over sixty different nationalities.

There were regular foreign correspondents, who resided in Beirut to cover the Middle East and who routinely met at the bar to exchange views and news. Second came the pundits – news editors, syndicated columnists and television and radio personalities – who occasionally stopped at the bar when they covered the Middle East as a part of their worldwide responsibility, their global beat. Then came the 'special correspondents', who appeared to report a specific story – a flare-up in the Arab-Israeli conflict, a coup d'état in a neighbouring country, the assassination of an Arab leader. There were also the local Lebanese journalists who worked for Beirut newspapers or for local bulletins with a special clientele – armament companies, the oil industry and the like. Some, of course, were spy-journalists.

A list of the bar press of the fifties, sixties and seventies would read like a who's who in journalism. Among the resident correspondents were Peter Jennings of ABC, Larry Collins of UPI and *Newsweek*, Erik de Mauney of the British Broadcasting Corporation (BBC), Kim Philby of the *Observer* and *The Economist*, Gavin Young of the *Guardian* and Bill Touhy of the *Los Angeles Times*. The pundits included Joe Alsop, C. L. Sulzberger, John Chancellor, Sefton Delmer, Henry Luce, Blair Frazer and Mohammed Hasanein Heikal. Among the people who arrived on special assignment were Larry Burrows and Hank Walker, David Brinkly, Jonathan Dimbleby, Peter Worthington and dozens of others. The local contingent included Marc Riashi, Hanna Ghossun, Afif Tibi, Fuad Ittayem, Salim Nassar.

For my father, Abu Saïd, a regular for twenty-five years while working for the *New York Times*, *Newsweek* and *Time*, the bar was the centre of the journalistic universe. He used it to meet colleagues, Lebanese politicians, exiles and visitors from other Arab countries, businessmen, spies, personal friends and anyone of importance. When I asked him whether the bar's existence mattered at all, he answered that it did, that some stories would never have been broken or would have died from neglect but for the bar, such as 'the political feuds among members of the Saudi royal family and King Hussein's conspiracies with the CIA'. According to him, some major news stories resulted when a disgruntled party knew where to spill the beans – namely, the bar.

When in the Middle East working for UPI and *Newsweek*, the young, astute Larry Collins used the bar selectively and effectively to exchange views with older, more seasoned colleagues. He learned through others' experience and he would tirelessly float ideas to gauge their reactions. He had come to the Middle East as an inexperienced novice but, through appreciation of what the bar had to offer, became a tried, reliable Middle East hand in a relatively short time.

Jonathan Randall of the *Washington Post* did not head-quarter in the bar like my father, but he used it for both news-gathering and verification. He talked to the bar staff to gauge local feelings and teased information out of spies in an attempt to decipher the doings of the intelligence community. He paid proper attention to the views of his colleagues and thoughts of Lebanese politicians; he used his excellent antennae well.

Bill MacLaughlin of CBS was cast from the Randall mould, a man who enjoyed 'getting the feel of what was happening in the Middle East – the bar was an excellent barometer'. He describes the bar as 'a small Middle East'.

Seasoned BBC correspondent Erik de Mauney always included the bar in his rounds, regarding it as a vital component in a very complex picture, a place where you heard some things, verified others and gave news its proper weight. There was always someone at the bar who knew about the latest rumour or who could explain its meaning.

Exceptionally, the resident correspondents were knowledgeable, hardworking, honest, ethical people who shared one thing: they were all heavy drinkers. The competitiveness among the journalists who saw each other there almost daily was elevating. True, *Time* wanted to beat *Newsweek*, the *Daily Mail* to out-do the *Daily Express* and NBC to scoop CBS, but it was also true that the bar press sat in judgement on the quality of its members' work and the methods each used on a daily basis. No group could officially ostracize anyone for misbehaviour, but the approval or disapproval of one's colleagues mattered. (One *Daily Mail* correspondent who unjustifiably exaggerated a story could not find a colleague to drink with for weeks.)

The pundits aimed to analyse, explain and occasionally propose solutions with an overall eye on regional developments – a far cry from the normal, day-to-day reporting concerns of resident correspondents. All of the visiting pundits – syndicated columnists Alsop and Sulzberger, *Daily Express* chief of correspondents Sefton Delmer, *Maclean's Magazine*'s foreign editor, Blair Frazer, and NBC's overall guru, John Chancellor – used resident journalists to bring them up to date; visited diplomats and local politicians to get the feel of things; quizzed spies, waiters and taxi drivers; and finally placed their local findings in the context of their own knowledge of the world.

For example, Alsop evaluated what he learned against his background of having information about policies originating in Washington, D.C., where he lived, worked and consorted with four presidents and many US secretaries of state. In the bar he was haughty, imperious and impatient, expecting everyone to wait on him, mercilessly questioning everyone over his favourite vintage wine. The victims of his relentless interrogation called him 'God almighty Alsop', but there could be no question that what he did was in the service of his higher aim: to produce a true picture of how things were.

Sulzberger was the same, but much gentler. Though he generated less noise than Alsop, his probing was no less purposeful, perhaps more methodical and cunning. His incisive reporting reflected a keen understanding of Russia's attitude towards the Middle East. Because his column was syndicated by the *New York Times*, Sulzberger often found himself asked to explain his points of view to the local *Times* man.

Sefton Delmer was preoccupied with the human element of what happened in any country. As a leading expert on psychological warfare, he saw events in terms of a battle for people's minds and hearts, just as he had when he was head of Britain's Psychological Warfare Executive (also known as Black Propaganda) during the Second World War. Even a conversation with the shoe-shine man would be projected against this bigger screen. This meant he sometimes read too much into too little – he did tend to exaggerate the communist threat to the Middle East.

Blair Frazer, as much a bar regular and journalist as any American or Briton, found he had a certain freedom as a Canadian. Unencumbered by allegiance to a country with vested interests in the Middle East, his neutrality endeared him to those reluctant to speak to British, American and even Russian journalists and enabled him to avoid partisan reporting. He exercised the outsider's privilege of rendering moral judgement and some of his reports thus concentrated unevenly on the misconduct of the major powers, as when he reported that 'no major power has a Middle East policy'.

John Chancellor was the youngest member of this group, and his approach was the freshest, the most personal and the friendliest. His populist streak made others relax in his presence, speak to him as a friend, trust him and, in the end, give him better interviews. He would then turn his populist streak around and use it to make the most complex events intelligible to the folks back home in Iowa or Idaho, as when he said: 'On the eastern shores of the Mediterranean there is a small country called Lebanon which is half Moslem and half Christian and the two sides don't like each other.'

The bar press handed the Middle East on a plate to the visiting pundits and they used it well. But the most bizarre use, or rather abuse, of the bar was by the special correspondents sent to the Middle East to cover a specific story, usually either representing a news organization which could not afford a permanent Middle East correspondent or reporting back to countries where the reader's interest in the area was limited to news of major flare-ups. These correspondents included newspapermen from Sacramento to Seattle and TV men from Cincinatti, as well as the odd Australian, Swedish or Finnish newsman. In most cases, they approached the bar as a student approaches a total-immersion, intensive course in an entirely new subject, in this case the Middle East. Lebanese journalist Hanna Ghossun has cynically observed that 'they came to the bar to become instant experts on the Middle East; I should have charged them a fee for talking to them.'

The special correspondents and their news organizations rarely had an adequate background for reporting on the Middle East. One such representative, perhaps on the strength of a single conversation with a bar writer, described the Baath Party which rules in Syria and Iraq as 'a Moslem party' – a grave error indeed in view of this political movement's secular attitude and its mostly Christian leadership. Another special correspondent sat in the bar among the seasoned experts and crudely asked, 'Why do the Arabs hate the Americans so much?'. (One of his more knowledgeable colleagues replied, 'It ain't that simple.') An Australian reporter who should not have been allowed west of Perth sat in the bar and stated emphatically that 'everything in Israel is better than here'. It's a wonder he didn't get lynched.

In his long years at the bar my father saw special correspondents come and go. Not only was Abu Saïd shocked at their ignorance, but he also deplored the reason which brought them there, namely their news organizations' desire to speak of their own man on the spot. He was not alone in recommending a dependence on news agency reporting; news agencies usually have good, experienced people.

Unfortunately, the ignorant arrogance of the bad special correspondent was shared by a very small group of bar regulars who should have known better, but who maintained a disdainful, neo-colonial attitude which totally ignored local peoples' feelings and aspirations. How could anyone who hates the Middle East and the Arabs possibly ever be a good correspondent there?

Most of the neo-colonialists were Britons unable to abandon the ways of the Empire. David Holden of *The Times* did not hate the Arabs, but he always behaved as if he was bored with them and talked down to them, which helped neither his cause nor that of *The Times*. Colonel John Slade-Baker of the *Sunday Times* offensively addressed bar waiters as 'boy'. When the *Sunday Times* recalled him, he told bar regulars how he visited the various Arab heads of state and, totally misunderstanding Arab hospitality, asked each for something to remember them by. He returned home with a collection of gold watches, but missed the looks of wonder on the faces of his hosts.

Henry Taylor, Jr, the very American correspondent of Scripps-Howard newspapers, thought that reading the *Koran* would improve his understanding of the area. He bought a copy but then, to the horror of all, brought it with him to the bar, stuck it in his back pocket and sat on it. An equally insensitive American wire service reporter asked concierge

Mansour Breidy to transmit a cablegram which contained the sentence 'in this backward part of the world'. Breidy refused to oblige.

I cannot but believe that these neo-colonialist reporters did considerable harm. Ali Bitar still reddens at the memory of Slade-Baker's calling him 'boy' and I still find the Taylor incident grossly offensive. If one accepts the premise that sensitivity to the world around serves a correspondent well, then these people were bad reporters.

Finally, there were the journalist-spies, those who used journalism as cover for their espionage activity. Some of them carried out their spying activity undetected and thus remained unknown, but this discussion only deals with those who have been exposed or uncovered. Some journalists spied with their employers' knowledge, while others did not have the consent of their news organizations to be used for cover.

The *Observer* and *The Economist*, Kim Philby's employers, profess a genuine ignorance of his spying activities. It is highly doubtful that the Italian news agency Continentale knew that Kheiry Hammad, their Middle East correspondent, was a spy for Nasser. On the other hand, a major American news weekly knowingly sent a major CIA spy to Beirut to head its Middle East bureau. A leading London daily has steadfastly refused to answer my questions about their Middle East correspondent of the early sixties, a man who made no secret of his special interest in Russian submarine use of Syrian port facilities, while managing totally to neglect dozens of newsworthy stories.

It is worth noting that all the cases of spies posing as bar journalists took place relatively recently, well after the clear division between the two professions was established earlier this century. So while the function and purpose of the two disciplines are no longer interchangeable, these examples and others confirm the commonly held belief that journalism is a good cover for spying.

We do not know whether Philby used the bar to spy, but he did use it as a journalist. Its use enhanced his journalistic credentials, which in turn probably made him a more effective

41

spy. Kheiry Hammad most definitely used his journalistic presence in the bar to recruit. A *Time* magazine correspondent showed special interest in Iraqi exiles, whom he met and debriefed at the bar. He was later exposed as a spy – his nominal job facilitated his real job. The correspondent from the London daily did not do much to hide his real function, but his reporter's credentials made it possible for him to enter Syria to check on his favourite story.

To confuse journalism with spying is harmful in practical, everyday ways. When Ali Bitar spoke of the Philby defection and exposure, he observed 'we became extra careful after Mr Kim disappeared; we didn't know whether people were journalists or spies'. Even politicians will shun journalists if they suspect them of spying. What is worse, the conflict of loyalties can lead to misreporting, both by commission and by omission. Then there is the all-important business of endangering colleagues' lives. The *Time* magazine spy recruited an important Iraqi to work for him. When the Iraqi was captured, tried and tortured, he gave the names of everyone he had met at the bar before his execution. Iraq had no claim on the foreigners on the confessional list, who were merely barred from entering the country, but locals, Arabs, were tried *in absentia* and sentenced to death. Among them was my father who, in his own words, 'would rather work for the Mafia than the CIA'.

Journalists of all types made constructive use of the bar. How they behaved under the influences of what the place had to offer can be seen by examining specific case studies.

Larry Collins, all on his own representing UPI, had to compete with an AP office of five correspondents. His judicial use of the bar as an information centre served him well. With a clear eye to the stories unfolding in the area, he established contacts with bar regulars who were close to these stories and secured their permanent help in keeping him informed every time something happened in their areas of expertise. As a result, he reported the US Marines' 1958 landing in Lebanon hours ahead of his competitors, uncovered a serious plot to overthrow King Hussein and was among the first to publicize the important Russian-Iraqi agreement to repatriate exiled Kurds and temporarily end a festering rebellion.

John Cooley, the Middle East correspondent of the *Christian Science Monitor* in the sixties, produced some of the finest long-range analysis of what was happening in the area. Cooley used the bar discreetly and well; his knowledge of the area enabled him to pursue some bar rumours and discard many others. What he heard in the bar from self-serving exiles and others allowed him to trace the perpetually shifting alliances in the Middle East with amazing clarity.

The use of the bar by people with a story to tell is best illustrated by what happened to Jonathan Randall of the *Washington Post* two days after the October 1973 War. A suspected British agent told Randall how the Egyptians crossed the Suez Canal by hosing down sand-built Israeli fortifications. Randall, along with others, had been occupied with determining the secret of the Egyptians' success. But he nodded politely and dismissed what he heard as an 'unlikely story' and missed one of the biggest scoops of the century. For reasons which remain unknown, MI6 was trying to get the story out.

Prince Tallal of Saudi Arabia was more successful than Randall's informer. His Highness, after consulting his aides on how to proceed, sent a special messenger to the bar carrying a sealed envelope which contained an important news story in the fullest detail. The Prince's documents revealed the existence of the free princes, members of the Saudi royal family who opposed their own government and brother Kind Saud, and who supported his enemy President Nasser of Egypt. According to Prince Tallal, their goal was to force Kind Saud to step down and to replace him with a militant, more anti-Israeli government friendly to Nasser. The envelope was delivered to my father two years before Saud abdicated; Abu Saïd scooped the world because HRH Prince Tallal knew where to find him.

Even the sense of camaraderie among the bar press contributed to better journalism. Older, experienced correspondents – such as de Mauney of the BBC, Izzard of the *Daily*

Mail, Don Burke of *Life* and John Mecklin of *Time*, all old-fashioned foreign correspondents who took pride in their profession – generously took the time to advise and help their younger colleagues and prided themselves in the achievements of their protégés. Don Burke once advised me not to go out on a limb until I was 'a hundred per cent sure; ninety-five per cent sure isn't enough'. Mecklin hired Tom Streithorst to work for *Time* and taught him the writing trade over drinks at the bar. The inherent sense of camaraderie elevated young reporters' professional standards, to the benefit of their readers and listeners.

This sense of professional pride extended beyond helping colleagues to include jealous protection of the press as a free institution; the bar press protected its own. American photographer Paul Davis clearly exceeded the accepted limits when he hired a boat and tried to reach and board the yacht of the Aga Khan, which was moored in St George Bay. But when the Lebanese police roughed him up, the bar press protested as one. When the CIA's John Fistere attempted to stifle reports of corruption in Jordan by casting aspersions on the characters of Denis Fodor of *Time* and myself, who had reported incidents of such misdeeds in Jordan, he was discredited by an angry bar press, which felt obliged to defend its enterprising members. *Time*'s Lee Griggs and Abu Saïd went out of their way to secure a residence permit for their colleague and competitor, the correspondent of *Newsweek*, because they thought he should have one. To guard the quality of its reporting, the bar press freely exchanged information about unreliable tipsters and visiting politicians with self-serving claims. One Lebanese charged a hefty fee for taking correspondents to record the sounds of battle, which were in reality a group of his friends who fired in the air when he gave them the signal. But he had no more takers after NBC exposed him to the rest of the bar press.

When Joe Alsop came to town, he would consult every resident journalist who mattered, often gathering them around him and acting as discussion group leader. He would seek out a local Lebanese journalist to check on local happenings or insist on talking to Iraqis about Iraq; he berated CIA agents when they tried to mislead him and told a high-level US embassy official who waffled instead of informing not to waste his time. He once summoned me and asked 'Saïd, tell me, what do the young people of this part of the world want?' One minute into my monologue, he interrupted: 'I know how they feel – I want to know what they want, do they know that?' I couldn't answer.

The Alsops of this world took over where the resident journalists left off. For years, the local press liked to refer to Arab refugees wishing to reclaim their land in Palestine as 'disillusioned'. It took John Chancellor to correct that; to him they were 'illusioned' – they knew exactly what they wanted. Canadian Blair Frazer listened to a Lebanese politician for two hours and left. He later told us, 'One of you local guys ought to tell the son of a bitch Lebanon isn't the centre of the universe, there are other considerations to be taken into account.' The bar had everything these big men needed in order to learn, examine and report a story. With all these elements at their fingertips they performed a superior job.

The interaction between the journalists and the spies and businessmen who used the bar was a question of smooth, two-way cooperation; each side used each other effectively. For example, Paul Parker of the Bank of America (later of Wells Fargo) was an excellent source of information for bar journalists wishing to assess financial and business developments in the Middle East. Conversely, his discreet exchanges with members of the bar press yielded valuable information which he incorporated in his analyses of future business prospects in the region. Kamel Abdel Rahman, chairman of Contracting and Construction Company (CCC), was the first man to appraise Libya's emergence as a major oil producer. Kamel gave this good story with far-reaching consequences to the bar press in order to enchance his position with the publicity-seeking Libyan government of the time. Saudi billionaire Suleiman Olayan, a much bigger and infinitely more discreet business figure than the infamous Adnan Khashogi, always stopped at the bar to benefit from its press insight on how the world viewed the Middle East. Someone eventually caught on and wrote Olayan's colourful life story. Getty Oil Co. general manager Ed Brown generated more than casual interest. An accomplished Arabist who was educated at Harvard and Cambridge, and an authority on the oil business as well as on Mr Getty's exotic life, Brown also traded information with discreet journalists who had something to tell him.

Perhaps the most obvious businessman user of the bar and its press was Emile Bustani, the father of Myrna, a Lebanese politician *par excellence*. An MIT graduate and a man of considerable wit and charm, Bustani came to the bar when he had something to say, his every appearance at the bar an instant mini-press conference. What Bustani had to say made excellent copy, but he was amazingly clever in how he did it and in deflecting questions he didn't want to answer. He never forgot the name of a single journalist with whom he spoke. He always left us feeling indebted to him – though more often than not he was the beneficiary of these forays into press land.

The reciprocity between journalists and spies was less obvious, but in many ways more important. We have already mentioned the use of the *New York Times* by the CIA and cases where newsmen and news organizations covered for intelligence operations, and there were, as in the case of Randall and the MI6 man, times when espionage organizations divulged secrets to the press. Intriguing as these episodes may be, it is much more important to know whether intelligence services misled the bar press and, through them, the world by manipulating the news with selective disclosures, outright fabrications or simple embellishments. The following chapter will deal with major cases of this type, which were serious enough to distort our view of the modern history of the Middle East. Everyday examples, however, are at the heart of the relationship between these two professions.

One way to distort news is the age-old trick of undermining the press' confidence in news-makers; when successful, it is eventually reflected in the type of press coverage they receive.

The bar CIA did an outstandingly sordid job of trying to undermine Dag Hammerskjøld, the late secretary-general of the United Nations, and one of his senior employees, William Clark, director general of the United Nations Relief and Work Agency (UNRWA) in Jordan. The austere, aristocratic Swede was considered unsympathetic to Israel and Clark, a British gentleman of the old school, was charged with the more specific crime of allowing anti-Israeli teaching in Palestinian refugee camps.

The bar CIA shamelessly tried to spread stories about both men's homosexuality. This piece of dirty-work was considered so important that the regular contingent of bar CIA men was reinforced by men who came from the American Embassy equipped for this purpose with every bit of dirt short of pictures – obviously there was a plan to force Clark to resign and to detract from Hammerskjøld's international reputation. The bar press, mostly for reasons of honour, did not act on these stories – if indeed they were stories. Both men survived the mud-slinging and Clark stayed in his post until his retirement in the late sixties. The attempt to discredit – for that's what it was – failed.

In one highly successful operation, British Intelligence leaked, then used, a piece of information to justify the 1959 landing of the Royal Marines in Kuwait. Iraq, then ruled by dictator Abdel Karim Kassem, had claimed Kuwait as part of its territory and declared its intention eventually to annex it. The Iraqi claim fell short of a direct threat, but the British government was determined to serve notice of its opposition to Iraq's plans because they feared for their substantial oil interests in Kuwait.

A British Intelligence officer operating under cover as an oil executive very cleverly met a British member of the bar press, a correspondent for a leading London daily newspaper who himself had suspect connections with MI6. The result was a scoop for the correspondent, a lead story which stated that Iraq's army was heading for Kuwait and contained the names of the units involved and their strength. The story caused a stir in London, particularly after other bar journalists followed the lead. The British government, to all intents and purposes responding to an immediate threat, landed a contingent of Royal Marines in Kuwait.

In reality there was no military danger to Kuwait and the British government knew it. True, Iraq's army units had moved out of Baghdad, but they had headed north to fight Kurdish rebels, not south to invade Kuwait. The British government had needed a pretext to wave the flag and orchestrated the whole phoney story with considerable success.

The powerful prince sultan of Saudi Arabia, full brother of King Fahd, Minister of Defence and second in line to the throne, frequented the bar in the sixties and regaled its bar press with stories about how the world financial system would be unbalanced by his country hoarding its huge oil revenues. In fact, his country was then run by the frugal King Faisal, who was deeply concerned about the effects of sudden wealth on the country and its social cohesion. Faisal's tight grip on the purse cramped the style of the spendthrift sultan and his cohorts, the like of arms dealer Adnan Khashogi, who wanted Faisal to spend more so they could make more. The bar press viewed the sultan's refrain with considerable misgiving, much as they viewed everything else he said and did.

Getting no satisfaction from the bar press, the sultan took his complaint to the CIA. Here the response was different, because the CIA and the US government also favoured the recycling of Saudi funds, preferably through its purchase of American goods. Two CIA agents came to the bar amply loaded with statistics demonstrating the adverse results of Faisal's policy and advocating a spending spree. One of them was Joseph Ellender, nominally an Aramco executive.

The ensuing press campaign in favour of greater Saudi spending led to a partial change in policy. That the US and the CIA have consistently advocated the spending, even squandering, of oil wealth is one of the sadder unreported facts of modern Middle Eastern history. The unfortunate results of this foolish, short-sighted approach are visible in the social dislocation wracking the Arabian Peninsula and in the destructive, wealth-induced pace of change which has created an unbridgeable generation gap, which seems centuries wide.

The wool was also pulled over the eyes of the bar press when it had as its hero a loud, gregarious CIA agent and bar regular who hired a blabbermouth of an Australian secretary to help with the memoirs of his exploits in Egypt. His so-called memoirs were deliberately filled with misleading information which the secretary whispered to any willing listener at the bar. Among the lies the secretary spread was the claim that some of Nasser's closest associates worked for the CIA. The information was recycled through the bar press and some of it eventually got back to Nasser, who imprisoned two of those named, who were, in reality, wholly anti-American.

The ways in which the bar press operated tell us a great deal about the workings of foreign reporting. I approached this subject with a critical eye, fearful that my findings might be negative, thereby endangering both my life-long love affair with journalism and valued relationships with its institutions and practitioners. I am happy to report that my study of one of the all-time great gathering-places of foreign correspondents and journalists, for the most part, has uncovered a happy story. I am full of unashamed admiration for the quality of reporting produced by the Alsops, Delmers, Sulzbergers and Chancellors of this world.

This rare admiration embraces even the resident foreign correspondents, the permanent bar press. Exceptionally, they did their work well and, in the process, confronted problems which we do not hear about. When Denis Fodor criticized corruption in Jordan, he knew he was putting his job on the line because King Hussein was near and dear to his employer, *Time*. Jonathan Randall may have missed one of the biggest scoops of all time, but he behaved honourably every step of the way; he refused to use a suspect story or to rely on a suspect source of information. John Cooley, at considerable risk to his position, championed the cause of the

Palestinians long before it became fashionable; his way was difficult, but he firmly believed he was right. In the sixties, Michael Adams of the *Guardian* prophesied a Middle East in constant, wrenching turmoil. This did not endear him to anyone; he paid a heavy price for his pessimism. Now we know he was right.

I remember when photographers Jim Pringle and Larry Burrows woke up at five in the morning to take 'the right' picture. And then there was the time my father was caught up in cross-fire between the Lebanese army and rebel ranks. Larry Collins, Paul Davis and I rushed out of Beirut to Damascus, trekked to the Iraqi border, then, on finding it closed, swung north to Turkey, proceeded to eastern Turkey in a taxi cab and then found ourselves forced to re-enter Syria before finally returning to our Beirut home base after three sleepless nights. We improvised every step of the way and came back empty-handed because Iraq was closed to all foreigners. All such manifestations of hard work and dedication go hand-in-hand with the glamour invested in the foreign correspondent's job.

Most foreign correspondents make occasional mistakes in fact and judgement. But the mistakes are honest ones, part of being human. When these errors arise because someone has been misleading them, using them, they never forgive those who duped them and very often make the latter pay a high price for their misdeeds.

Having studied corruption in the Middle East and published my disturbing findings in 1985 (*Pay-Off: Wheeling and Dealing in the Middle East*), I have more than the usual preoccupation with this subject. But I can categorically state that in a part of the world where bribery is a way of life, I have not unearthed a single instance where a foreign correspondent succumbed to the temptation of bribery, though I know dozens of offers which have been made. Many of them would not accept so much as a drink from someone they did not know or when they thought that they could not reciprocate.

My one major criticism concerns the use of journalism by

the intelligence community as cover in any way, whether by individual journalists or with the sanction of an organization. It is deplorable, dangerous and destructive. The *New York Times*, often accused by right-wing elements in the US of harbouring KGB agents, should have discovered Brewer's total reliance on the CIA and put an end to it. *Time* magazine should know better than to front for the CIA and the British journalist who did MI6's dishonest work in fabricating the pretext for the landing in Kuwait did foreign reporting considerable harm. Like others, I am at a loss to describe Kim Philby's use of the *Observer* and *The Economist*, except to say that the end result was damaging to both publications and British journalism, though Kim was a most able journalist who saw beyond the blinding details of everyday events and addressed issues of lasting significance. Certainly the London daily whose correspondent spent well over a year at the bar without writing a word should be punished – perhaps its foreign correspondents' credentials should not be accepted.

This nagging area aside, the bar press was a great fraternity whose members met the highest standards of decency and enterprising journalism. I am proud and exceptionally privileged to have been a junior member of this group.

4

THE TRUTH EMERGES

When he wrote what is perhaps the definitive book on foreign reporting, *The First Casualty (The War Correspondent as Hero, Propagandist and Myth-Maker)*, Philip Knightley avoided the Middle East altogether. Because the Middle East of the twentieth century suffered more wars than any other part of the world, this amazing and very disturbing omission detracts from an otherwise excellent effort. In my view, there have been more instances of distortion of the truth in reporting by the press in the Middle East than in any other part of the world, and this is true of those who used the bar, for twenty-five years the centre for journalists covering that still-turbulent part of the world. My strong opinion raises two immediate questions: why is the Middle East rife with such misreporting, and how do I reconcile this fact with my open admiration for journalists who operated there, the ones who used the bar?

There are four major battles behind the news from today's Middle East: the Arab-Israeli conflict, the confrontation between East and West, the never-ending tension between the haves and the have-nots and the clash of resurgent Islamic fundamentalism with the twentieth century. There are endless variations of alignment between these forces, greater than anything facing journalists elsewhere. The mere act of reducing the endless variables to traceable patterns is extremely difficult and can lead to misreporting. Kuwait's position, for example, is riddled with contradictions: it is Arab and hence anti-Israeli, but pro-West and therefore an ally of Israel's ally; it is Moslem but anti-Iranian, capitalist but with an elaborate welfare system, and so on. As if each nation's internal contradictions were not enough, correspondents are expected to report the Middle East as a single entity, one place, reconciling the policies of some twenty individual countries.

To further complicate the problem of accurate reporting, Russia, the US, Israel, Britain, France, Saudi Arabia, Egypt, Iraq and Iran, to mention only a few players, have propaganda machines to promote their version of Middle East events. Even far-away Brazil, now a major arms supplier to the area, has gone into the business of twisting the truth. India, constantly at odds with Pakistan, has an elaborate propaganda machine aimed at limiting Middle Eastern Islamic support for its arch-enemy.

The Middle East is thus fertile ground for truth-twisting: its story is complex and there are dozens of versions of it. Reporting from the bar was perhaps more vulnerable than from other Middle Eastern spots because it was a centre for propagandists and self-serving exiles as well as for journalists. The truth of major news stories could easily be different, or more complex, than 'the first draft of history' presented in the reports which immediately followed events and which established them in people's minds.

Henry J. Taylor, Jr, of Scripps-Howard Newspapers, went to Jordan with an introduction to Radi Abdallah, who was in 1959 King Hussein's military aide-de-camp and trusted friend. The autumn of 1959 was a particularly difficult time for King Hussein, who was under pressure from Nasser to change his pro-Western policies and join Egypt in an Arab union. Hussein's position was insecure because his own people admired Nasser and believed in his dream of Arab unity.

Taylor wanted to interview Hussein; the king's precarious position was a big story. His downfall would affect the balance of power in the Middle East, endangering the West's strategic position and oil interests. Taylor stopped in at the bar in preparation for his trip to Amman, and there the Jordanian military attaché in Lebanon advised him to see Radi Abdallah, His Majesty's military aide-de-camp, who could organize an interview with Hussein. Two days after taking in all the bar had to offer on Jordanian affairs, Taylor took the one-hour flight to Amman, happy in the thought that this introduction to such a close and important friend of the king was likely to facilitate his mission.

An edgy, agitated Henry Taylor appeared in Beirut a day later, fully convinced that he possessed a story much bigger than the one he had been pursuing. He had called Abdallah upon his arrival in Amman to be told 'Colonel Abdallah is under arrest for conspiring to overthrow the monarchy. His Majesty will be holding a press conference to divulge the details of the conspiracy in two days.' Taylor was on top of a major scoop, which he automatically shared with Larry Collins of UPI because of the mutual cooperation connection between UPI and Scripps-Howard and with me because I had introduced him to the military attaché. This was an excellent story for the wire services and the daily newspapers, even a good one for my employer, Radio Free Europe.

Taylor, Collins and I reviewed the story in the bar and went our separate ways to write it, attaching our own interpretations. There were headlines and a 'well done' congratulatory cablegram from Radio Free Europe. The rest of the bar's press corps rushed to Amman to cover His Majesty's press conference, where Hussein, almost in tears, told the world of the perfidy of his almost 'most trusted aide', lamented his inability to trust anyone and attacked Nasser for sponsoring attempts on his life.

The world was full of sympathy for the brave boy-king, all except for three bar regulars and Suheil Abu Hammad, an occasional visitor. The first regular was an agent of the CIA who simply knew better. The second, Sam Brewer of the *New York Times*, was bothered by Hussein's generalities and the fact that the plot seemed to lack one necessary ingredient – the inclusion of other army officers. The third, Abu Saïd, knew Hussein and Abdallah and their relationship, and refused to believe it. Suheil Abu Hammad had good reason to be suspicious.

Abdallah was kept under house arrest for a year and a half without trial. Afterwards, he was released by Hussein in what appeared to be an act of kindness towards an old friend. His release, rehabilitation and elevation to the post of Minister of the Interior went almost unnoticed. What actually happened was even more bizarre, another plot that never was. Hussein was not betrayed; on the contrary, he betrayed a friend to cover his own misdeeds, and, in the process, squeezed in some propaganda for himself against Nasser.

The CIA agent had given Hussein the sum of two million dollars for covert operations against Syria, then part of the United Arab Republic, founded by a merger of Egypt and Syria. The covert operations were to be specific sponsorships of anti-Nasser Syrians to cause explosions and perhaps public disturbances, demonstrations and riots. The money was deposited at Chase Manhattan Bank in Beirut, where Suheil Abu Hammad worked. Hussein and Abdallah, who doubled as his trusted intelligence chief, were the authorized signatories.

Hussein had no intention of using the money for its designated purpose; instead, he spent it. When this became apparent, the CIA man visited Amman several times, demanding that the money be returned. He would not accept no for an answer. A week before Abdallah's arrest, Hussein confided to the agent that Abdallah had gambled the money away and promised to do something about it. He did not limit himself to accusing Abdallah of embezzlement, but also successfully realized mileage from the situation on the theory that the bigger the lie, the more it is believed. Abdallah had not led a conspiracy or gambled the money away, and he knew the reasons for his arrest.

Collins, Taylor and I had acted honourably. We were presented by a statement from a popular king which left us no alternative but to treat it with the importance it deserved. Our inexperience showed when, unlike Brewer, we failed to notice the absence of co-conspirators; nor did we possess Abu Saïd's educated, discerning sense of the improbable. It was also a text book example of how to influence the press. I cannot verify what the *New York Times* did when Brewer filed corrections to this large but untrue story, but *Time* magazine decided correcting an old story wasn't worth a line. Hussein, a master manipulator of the media, got away with it. Even the CIA toed the line; they not only wrote off the money, but they supported Hussein's story because they saw in it a chance to prop up his shaky régime.

Misleading the media was and remains an intrinsic CIA function, particularly outside America. During the 1968–69 period, CIA agents using the bar managed to sell different versions of the same story to no less than ten different news organs, including the *New York Times*, *Newsweek*, the *Daily Mail* and *Le Monde*. The basic story was a simple one: Russia was arming rebellious Kurds to seek autonomy in northern Iraq against the central government in Baghdad. Because Russia professed friendship towards Iraq, this was presented as an example of Russian perfidy, certainly a clear warning to anyone in the Middle East who believed in Russia's ostensibly pro-Arab foreign policy.

The stories described the leader of the Kurds, Mulla Mustapha Al Barazani, the Red Mulla, giving details of the arms the Russians sent to him and speaking elaborately of Russian plans to create a Kurdistan, a new country comprising parts of Iraq, Iran and Turkey. The story gained added credibility when a successful Iraqi army offensive against the rebellious Kurds led to the capture of hundreds of prisoners fully equipped with Russian hardware. The Iraqis, believing they were in possession of evidence to support the claims of the Western press, summoned the Russian ambassador and protested strongly. They even considered severing diplomatic relations.

Sefton Delmer, the psychological warfare expert, was in the bar in early 1969 as part of a routine tour of the Middle East on behalf of a number of German publications. His inaugural stop at the bar had always served him well; this time he landed on top of a major disinformation story. A shadowy, unhappy figure in the corner of the bar found in Delmer exactly what he wanted – a major journalist with the authority to give his story the maximum exposure and impact. Delmer listened, checked and rechecked every detail of the story and his informer's background, then fearlessly ran with it. Arms dealers usually cut their losses when deals turn sour, but Delmer's jittery informer was dead set on revenge. The lonely little man told Delmer that the arms reaching the Kurds were part of a CIA-Israeli-Jordanian conspiracy to discredit Russia and its Middle Eastern policy.

The story as reported by Delmer went as follows: the Russian arms with which the Kurds were equipped came from Sinai, where they had been discarded by the retreating Egyptian army in the 1967 Arab-Israeli War, the Six-Day War. At the prompting of the CIA and with Israeli consent, the Jordanians sent bedouins across the Negev Desert into Sinai to collect the arms, bring them back to Jordan and then smuggle them to Iraq. The Kurds, too, were party to the plot, happily aware that it might lead to an Iraqi-Russian estrangement which would afford them a better chance of success. King Hussein's uncle, Sherrif Nasser bin Jamil, organized the operation, charging the CIA exorbitant prices for the Russian equipment, and then reneged on the payment to his partner, Delmer's desperate informer. The plot would have succeeded but for the greed of Sherrif Nasser and the arms dealer's suicidal inclinations.

In this case, the correction was worth it because the Kurdish rebellion was still in progress and the correction itself was a story. Because the publication date of a story determines its importance, the withholding of a usable story until any likelihood of damage to innocent people or to institutions worth protecting has passed is the ultimate act of journalistic statesmanship.

John Chancellor of NBC is an urbane, imperturbable journalist whose outward calm is a reflection of his inner makings. To Donald Gordon of the Canadian Broadcasting Corporation (CBC) and myself, the fellow who walked into the St George Hotel bar in the autumn of 1958 was not the man we had known. As happened very often, he joined us for a drink, but he was a man preoccupied, almost nervous.

After another drink, Chancellor revealed the source of his anxiety. He had just been to see Admiral Holloway, commander of the US Sixth Fleet and overall commander of the US forces which had landed in Lebanon in 1958 to prop up its shaky pro-Western government against Nasser-sponsored rebels who were trying to subvert it from within. Holloway had answered a telephone call while Chancellor was interviewing him aboard the aircraft carrier and excused himself to go out to see someone. Chancellor saw on the Admiral's desk, placed in a way so he couldn't miss it, the outline of a plan to kidnap Saeb Salam, the pro-Nasser Lebanese rebel leader. The plan called for a contingent of US marines to go to see Salam disguised as foreign correspondents and doing what was necessary after gaining entry through this cover.

The proposed use of this cover was extremely disturbing to Chancellor, let alone the consequences of the kidnapping under any guise. We all agreed that the plan could discredit US foreign correspondents for a long time to come, but none of us knew what to do. Chancellor had no way of knowing whether Holloway had meant for him to see the plan or whether Holloway's reputation for shallowness (he was unfondly known as Hollowhead) was deserved. But he decided to hold on to the story regardless.

Chancellor left Beirut after swearing Gordon and myself to secrecy. As I was doing the occasional radio spot for the CBC, Gordon and I had reason to meet at the bar almost daily. We were often short of broadcast stories, wondering aloud what to do for news material. The thought of betraying Chancellor's trust never occurred to us, nor did we discuss the matter in any way except to agree that Chancellor's must have been an accidental discovery, otherwise Holloway would have found another channel through which to tell the story.

Months later, on 2 January 1959, my photographer friend Harry Kondakjian walked into the bar with a copy of Beirut's afternoon daily *Al Youm* and announced to all journalists present that there had been a plot to kidnap Saeb Salam. Chancellor disclosed the story on the NBC end-of-year report. He had held on to it for months for reasons of honour, then broadcast it as a critique of the US government's short-sighted ways.

The least that could have happened if Chancellor had broadcast the story in time would have been the total discrediting of all US foreign correspondents, perhaps all foreign correspondents – even if the plan had not been carried out. It could have induced Nasser to increase his support to Lebanese rebels in anticipation of an attempt to kidnap their leader, thereby contributing to a cycle of escalation completely beyond anyone's control. It would have undermined the US position in Lebanon and the rest of the Arab world for years to come.

The lack of wisdom of those who devised such a foolish plan was met and neutralized by Chancellor's honesty. He placed US interest and the reputation of US journalism ahead of the temptations of a scoop. Rightly, he did not speak out until all potential damage had been offset by changes in the Lebanese political landscape and then, equally rightly, to forestall the potential future development of such idiotic plans. In this case, there was good reason to withhold the truth. Many years later, an equally important story was never reported because the news organizations which knew it lacked the courage of a Chancellor and the dedication of a Delmer; they put business considerations ahead of the truth.

The 1973 increase in oil prices and its effects on the world economy was one of the big news stories of the seventies. Prophets of gloom went so far as to predict the collapse of the Western economies. There was open talk of the military occupation of the oil fields and the enforcement of a sensible pricing policy on oil producers. Producers had pegged the price of OPEC oil at thirty-two dollars per barrel, but the price of the commodity on the open market shot up to forty-two dollars, ominously higher than the official price. The bar journalists were rightly occupied with reporting and analysing the situation against this background of an economic story which could lead to a depression or war. Even foreign correspondents who usually avoided economic stories were educating themselves in the intricacies of the mechanics of supply and demand and price elasticity.

Fuad Ottayem, the able, well-connected editor of the *Middle East Economic Digest* and a bar visitor, was the first to break the news of Saudi Arabia's decision to increase oil production to satisfy extra demand and force down prices. It was one of his many scoops and the bar press, as happened so many times during this period, followed Ottayem's lead. The sigh of relief which started in the bar reached the far corners of the globe.

Early in 1975 the messenger of a Saudi prince arrived in the bar from Saudi Arabia with one purpose in mind: to tell foreign journalists that while his country had adopted a policy aimed at lowering oil prices, individual members of the House of Saud had a vested personal interest in keeping these prices up, in order to line their pockets. According to this bar visitor, the additional Saudi production intended to change the supply-demand situation was to be marketed by Petromin, the state company in charge of this activity. Influential members of the House of Saud had divided the Petromin share and were following plans directed at maintaining high prices. In other words, the sensible policy of the Saudi government was being undermined by influential, greedy members of the royal family, who saw it as an opportunity to get richer.

It was remarkable for a new visitor to the bar to frequent it every day for a week. Curiosity surrounded the man, particularly when the connection between the visitor and the Saudi royal family had been established. He met most of the foreign correspondents and engaged them in friendly but conventional conversation while studying them, methodically keeping mental notes on their characters and the journalistic establishments they represented.

With time, the astute visitor seemed to concentrate on the correspondents of a leading London newspaper and an American financial daily, eventually opting to spill the beans first to the Englishman. The story was solidly documented with the names of the culprits, the amounts of oil they sold and the prices. Prince Mohamad bin Abdul Aziz of Saudi Arabia, a man who should have been king but for his drinking, was the leading guilty party, but there were other princes and higher-ups in the Saudi Ministry of Petroleum. His answer to the obvious question as to why he was disclosing all this was to label it 'an internal family matter'.

When the English journalist, after consulting with his editor in London, told the Saudi of their decision against using the story, the latter used his American option. Shockingly, the answer from the American financial daily was the same, and the amiable Saudi was forced to pack his bags and return to his country empty-handed. The reason for the newspapers' negative answers was one and the same: neither doubted the veracity of the story, but both preferred not to endanger their relationship with Saudi Arabia. Their common fears included the possibilities that their correspondents would be banned from entering the country and that their syndicated services would no longer be sold to Saudi newspapers.

This case represents a growing danger to honest reporting: the placement of the interests of 'the business' ahead of the commitment to telling the truth. 'I don't want to do anything to rock the boat' and 'if I do that I won't be able to go there again' are two sentences gnawing at the heart of enterprising journalism. While it is difficult to quantify, I am near certain that other bar regulars, the resident foreign correspondents covering the area, would also have chosen this unfortunate way, either on their own or under pressure from their editors.

Some of the crimes of misreporting have their origins in good intentions; they are honest mistakes or attempts to do what is right which backfire. They can be committed by the most experienced and knowledgeable of correspondents and often the mistake is compounded because the reputation of the correspondent involved gives it additional weight.

A.T. entered the bar very much like a man with a mission, a very specific mission which had brought him from Saudi Arabia especially to see the unelected dean of the foreign journalists, Abu Saïd of *Time* magazine. The two reserved for each other that particular type of affection homeless people have for each other. Both were Palestinians. True to form, my father came to the bar around noon. Ali Bitar quietly told him that A.T. had been waiting for him for half an hour and Abu Saïd, ever so careful not to keep anyone waiting, joined him right away. Effusive Arab greetings out of the way, the two entered what might be described as an animated whispering session.

A.T. had come directly to the bar as a result of a conversation with King Fahd of Saudi Arabia, who had just succeeded the benevolent, fatherly King Khalid to the throne. An unofficial adviser and sidekick to His Majesty, A.T. had been privy to discussions regarding the uncomplimentary journalistic stories which had been published on the latter's accession to the throne. A.T. claimed to have volunteered to put an end to the stories by coming to the bar to see his 'dear friend' Abu Saïd, who had considerable influence among the bar journalists who were filing the stories. Calling upon Abu Saïd's every iota of loyalty to Araby, A.T. particularly emphasized the need to champion King Fahd because of his, Fahd's, importance to the Palestinians and their cause. King Fahd had personally sanctioned the mission.

Abu Saïd was caught. Absolving himself from the contents of the reporting of others, some of whom sat within earshot in the bar, was easy, but there was a bigger, more immediate problem. *Time* was planning a cover story on the king and some of the material in it was likely to be critical, perhaps more harsh than the story already objected to by His Majesty and his emissary. Under the circumstances, running an unflattering cover story was tantamount to flouting the wishes of the king, practically spitting in his face.

The two made a date to meet in the bar at the same time the following day. Uncharacteristically, Abu Saïd needed time to think. He was not a stranger to controversy, but this unexpected situation was full of pitfalls. The happiness or otherwise of Abu Saïd's fellow Palestinians mattered little; what nagged him was whether Fahd, to whom he never ascribed far-sightedness, would consider *Time*'s criticism an act of betrayal by a Palestinian and would hold it against them as a group. In the end it was a responsibility Abu Saïd did not wish to assume.

The next day, occupying the same table of the bar as if they had never left it, the two men resumed their conversation of the day before. Abu Saïd made a feeble promise to try to talk to fellow journalists, but promised no results. He then told A.T. of the impending cover story on His Majesty and in this case promised to present Fahd in a favourable light.

The *Time* magazine cover story did not praise Fahd, but Abu Saïd managed to eliminate the damning part which had described Fahd as 'a gambler and a womanizer'. That was the extent of the balance between his conflicting loyalties to his employer and his people. Unhappily, Abu Saïd lived long enough to regret this accommodation. Months afterwards, news reached him that A.T. had told Fahd that he had had to buy Abu Saïd and received a substantial sum of money in return from the Saudi treasury. He never spoke to A.T. again and whether the Palestinians benefited from his efforts is highly doubtful. A.T.'s initial act was nothing more than blackmail, silencing people in the cause of a national interest that did not exist, a short step removed from attempts to kill my book about corruption in the Middle East, *Pay-Off* (including an offer from a Middle East government of £200,000 not to publish it). Both Abu Saïd and I regret the fact that he succumbed.

What does it all mean? The examples we have seen show King Hussein lying to the press in a deliberate, serious way and its young members subordinating good judgement to momentary success, the CIA with Israel and Jordan using the press to fabricate a situation which did not exist, John Chancellor withholding the truth to serve America and journalism, two papers in London and New York refusing to run a newsworthy story lest it endanger their business interests and an old, tried hand falling victim to good intentions and – perhaps – blackmail.

These examples demonstrate the vulnerability of foreign reporting to pressures and influences beyond the comprehension of the average reader or viewer. But, and it is an extremely important thing to remember, only one of these stories was beyond amendment or correction. The knowledge of King Hussein's outwitting the press was short-lived and he was never believed as before. Sefton Delmer blew the lid off the CIA's elaborate scheme at considerable cost to the participants. Chancellor's behaviour did more good than harm; the press benefited from his justified complaint. Abu Saïd's view of the corruption of Fahd's court was strengthened by its successful attempt to blackmail him. Only the question of stifling a story in favour of business interests remains beyond solution; something I leave for the academics of the communications business. A free press with the potential for self-correction is worthy of respect.

5

THE COUP THAT
NEVER WAS

Disinformation, a word very much in vogue, has not yet made it into the *Oxford English Dictionary*. But it is nevertheless a useful designation for an activity which is very much a part of our times: misleading through the dissemination of erroneous information or altering news to produce a false, favourable political picture. The practice of disinformation by Western intelligence organizations matured outside the boundaries of functioning democracies. In far-away places, the results of what amounts to official lying were – and are – not subject to the same sensitive standards and monitoring applied to domestic news.

The exposure of one such story involving the bar press – how its American, British and other members were manipulated by the CIA in a stunning success story of disinformation – is part of my purpose in this chapter. This particular story, a huge lie, is slowly finding its way into the history books, so the time to correct it has come.

The heroes of this particular gross misrepresentation of the truth are King Hussein of Jordan and the CIA (an organization with a long, sordid record of truth-twisting). Hussein, in spite of this and other lies, still has a very good image in the Western press, which makes this story doubly interesting; it shows that we act in accordance with our own lies.

In the summer of 1957 King Hussein was twenty-two; Jordan's population of two-and-a-half million was two-thirds of Palestinian origin; and Nasser was President of Egypt, pro-Russian and leader of the Arabs everywhere, particularly the Palestinians, who saw in him their best hope to defeat Israel. The US was extremely worried by Nasser's growing influence, which threatened to subordinate Jordan and other Arab countries to an unfriendly dictator.

Hussein and the US had Nasser as a common enemy. The clash between Nasser's dreams of one, big Arab country under himself and the US policy of supporting Arab leaders who favoured its policies was obvious, openly manifesting itself in a relentless propaganda war aimed at winning the hearts and minds of the Arab people. On the other hand, Hussein's opposition to Nasser was secret and highly personal, born from the wish to protect his throne without offending Nasser's followers by openly disagreeing with him. Even Jordan's freely elected cabinet, for the first and only time reflecting the will of the people, was pro-Nasser, an added reason for Hussein's reluctance to give battle.

This is the background to the CIA-Hussein conspiracy to rid Jordan of Nasser's influence and the reason behind the meetings in the corner of the bar between James Barracks of the CIA and Colonel Radi Abdallah, then Jordan's military attaché in Beirut, a man with a direct line to the young king. Barracks had settled for dealing with Abdallah in the bar because the situation in Jordan was not conducive to a visit. A personal meeting with Hussein could not have been kept secret because even people within Hussein's immediate entourage were pro-Nasser, likely informers on such a mission.

On the other hand, Abdallah's journeys to Amman and meetings with the king were in the line of duty, ostensibly routine, as was the case with military attachés in general. His bar meetings with Barracks, except for a level of frequency which went almost unnoticed, were almost ordinary, for the two men had long known each other; there was nothing strange in the freewheeling intelligence operative having the odd drink with someone of Abdallah's ilk. The one who had good reason to believe there was more to the meetings than met the eye was barman Ali Bitar, who took special interest in serving them personally after noting the length and frequency of the meetings.

The result of the Abdallah-Barracks têtes-à-têtes hit the

headlines in August 1957. London and US papers, followed by the press worldwide, featured stories claiming a Nasser conspiracy to dethrone Hussein. The story which filled the headlines for a week told how the brave boy-king foiled the sinister plot using army units loyal to him, personally leading them to victory, and how he dismissed Prime Minister Suleiman Nabulsi and Chief of Staff Ali Abu Nawar after discovering their complicity, dissolved parliament and declared a state of emergency.

Three days after his heroic daring deed to save his crown, King Hussein held a press conference in which he rehashed and embellished the history of the plot, adding a highly dramatic note by speaking of Nasser's perfidy after he, Hussein, had done everything possible to accommodate him, even to the extent of joining him in an anti-Israeli military alliance. Not a single reporter questioned Hussein's version of events; most of the bar press had gone to Amman to see him after being briefed by mysterious men from the American Embassy who had appeared at the bar with details of Nasser's shameful act. The story given by the Americans and Hussein's own account differed only in detail.

Writing for a weekly magazine, which allowed time for a closer look, *Time*'s John Mecklin and Abu Saïd were beginning to have doubts. Their initial unease was aroused by the sudden appearance in the bar of the Hussein promoters. Then Abdallah, a natural source of Jordanian news for them, went mysteriously missing. The Jordanian Embassy's telephone operator said the colonel was on leave, but later the doorman at the building where he lived told them that Abdallah had left for Amman with a tall, thin, bespectacled American, clearly Barracks, a man who never sought to conceal his CIA identity. Two days later the pieces began to fall in place when a reliable Jordanian with close connections to the dismissed Prime Minister Nabulsi told the investigating duo that 'There was no conspiracy – the premier definitely knew nothing about it.' Ali Bitar supplied the missing link when he retold disjointed snippets of conversation he had overheard when serving Abdallah and Barracks.

The first story filed by the *Time* bureau hedged its bets; it retold the news, including Hussein's press conference, but introduced an element of doubt into the conspiracy story by highlighting the neglected obvious: Nasser had no interest in overthrowing Hussein because such a move would invite Israeli reprisal, in all likelihood occupation of the West Bank, then under Jordanian control. The disclaimer went unnoticed except to the experienced journalistic eye, a concept too complex to overshadow the more obvious, appealing story of a colourful, pro-Western king in distress.

Having done all they could in Beirut, mostly at the bar, the *Time* correspondents headed to Jordan for a first-hand look at what was happening and, they hoped, an interview with Hussein for a cover story. In Amman they confirmed the presence of Barracks, who had been there since two days before 'the coup', staying at the palace with His Majesty, and Abdallah had been there as well. They discovered that certain Jordanian diplomats of doubtful loyalty to Hussein had been summoned home weeks before to arrive in Amman in time for arrest. Even lowly pro-Nasser people were arrested a few hours after the troubles had started; they had been earmarked by Hussein loyalists. All facts appeared clearly to point in the direction of a coup, not on behalf of Nasser but against his supporters.

The *Time* Hussein interview took place after these facts had been established, but a proud, cocky Hussein didn't concede much. His one step backward was to admit that, having expected his enemies to move against him, he had organized to meet this eventuality. *Time* turned the events in Jordan into its lead story and showed Hussein, military uniform and all, on the cover. Details of the CIA-Hussein cooperation were not reported in the story, but were used to convince *Time*'s editors of the soundness of their correspondents' findings. However, the story did dispel the anti-Hussein conspiracy report and went further; it said that it was a conspiracy led by Hussein against a freely elected government and strongly hinted at US complicity.

Hussein, flush with victory, was furious; he sent a

thinly disguised threat to Mecklin and Abu Saïd via his co-conspirator Radi Abdallah. Barracks re-surfaced in Beirut, more smug than ever, and came to the bar to lament the anti-Americanism of the *Time* report and provide all would-be listeners with stories supporting their original reporting. The bar press was in a state of civil war, divided between those who supported *Time* and those who stuck to their original story.

The British bar press was not its enterprising self; blinded by the Suez War fiasco, they supported anything anti-Nasser. Besides, Hussein was a graduate of Harrow and Sandhurst, one of their own. Even the local BBC man lost all sense of impartiality and openly condemned the Egyptian president, stopping just short of describing Hussein as heaven-sent. The *Daily Telegraph* went further: to the *Telegraph* it all went to prove the wisdom of Suez.

The one man who felt that his professional integrity was challenged by the *Time* article was columnist Joe Alsop. The Washington-based columnist had told his readers in over one hundred and fifty newspapers that there had been a genuine attempt on Hussein's life. He had returned to Washington from a quick trip to Amman and he had reported the whole affair in terms of the East-West confrontation in the Middle East and the need for the West to hold the line in the face of Russian expansionism. The *Time* story made a nonsense of the basis for his story, which he had checked and rechecked with his diplomatic and espionage sources. Either Mecklin and Abu Saïd had been misled, or he was made to look a fool.

An angry Alsop felt obliged to return to Beirut to settle the issue of right and wrong. After checking in at the hotel, he marched into the bar stormily with *Time*'s cover story in hand. Sighting Mecklin and Abu Saïd, he walked over to them, slammed the magazine on their table and shouted: 'Where the hell did you get this nonsense from? I demand an apology from both of you.'

As members of the bar press watched, Mecklin went uncharacteristically pale and silent. My father had to respond; the story was mostly his work. With as much of a smile as he could muster, he invited Alsop to join them, adding, 'I'll even buy you a drink.'

What followed was a bar dialogue between professional newsmen about their work and their assessment of their rôle. Out of respect for Alsop, the *Time* people supported every allegation they had made in their article with facts, time and sequence. They even went into the money paid to some Jordanian army officers to buy their loyalty to Hussein, but they refused to reveal sources. The information about Barracks and the US embassy boys who had acted as public relations officers for Hussein with the bar press seemed to disturb Alsop, who had known Barracks.

A day later, Alsop marched into the US Embassy in Beirut, in the words of a resident correspondent, 'to take the ambassador's head off'. The two men met, but nothing like that happened. Instead a chastened Alsop spent two days at the bar, did more reporting about the Middle East and went back to Washington without mentioning the story again.

Just about every book covering these events restates the original mistake and refers to an attempted coup against Hussein. Powerful as *Time* magazine was, and is, the reporting of that period followed the disinformation line developed by the CIA and executed by Barracks and Abdallah. They did not stop at organizing the phoney coup, or counter-coup; they realized the value of the power of the press from the start and briefed their lackeys on what to say, to whom and under what conditions.

Here the bar was used to hatch a major political plot, indeed a coup: both the misreporting of the event and its correction originated there. Even the confrontations between anti- and pro-Hussein journalistic factions (Alsop vs *Time*) took place there. Hussein aside, all the players were bar regulars: Abdallah, Barracks, Mecklin, Abu Saïd, Alsop, numerous foreign correspondents and the head waiter.

Coming relatively early in the life of the bar as a centre for journalists and spies, the circumstances surrounding this story helped enhance the reputation of the place. Foreign correspondents, getting a taste of what happened there, used it more than ever before, as did others with self-serving pieces of information or disinformation. *Time* magazine's efforts notwithstanding, this major piece of disinformation worked. Upset as he was about being duped, Joe Alsop opted to accept a line beneficial to US foreign policy. Sadly, British hatred of Nasser made the British press willing accomplices in a CIA operation embodying the type of lie they normally loved to criticize.

'Why didn't we pass the hat and get them a room to discuss US foreign policy in private?'

Time correspondent John Mecklin, on hearing two CIA agents discuss the Middle East in the bar

'So many of the people around the bar were spies. I am still suffering the after effects; I see spies everywhere.'

Abu Saïd

'What, a book about the St George Hotel bar . . . well, it sounds like the spying equivalent of the Algonquin Round Table.'

Win Levine

6
SPIES AND FRIENDS
– KIM PHILBY

The sight of the backs of Kim Philby, Bill Eveland and Kheiry Hammad as they stood next to each other at the bar was familiar to bar regulars, almost a daily occurrence. One day, as my father and I sat down for a pre-lunch cocktail, Abu Saïd aptly observed: 'We know they are all spies but we don't know for whom they work.' We both chuckled appropriately, but only a naive, spy-struck outsider would find anything peculiar about the presence of the three spies; they were familiar figures in a familiar game. Because they were also friends, one took the usual care and did not talk about their work. That would have been bad manners.

With the benefit of hindsight, and in the light of Philby's defection, the Hammad exposure and Eveland's autobiography, *Ropes of Sand*, my father's comment has gained weight; it goes to the heart of the matter. Obviously, the overall allegiance of bar spies to a specific country was important, but my father's maxim was meant to go further. Even when somebody's loyalty to country was beyond question, the particular connection within that nation's intelligence operation carried weight. So the question about Philby and Hammad concerned what country they worked for, but about Eveland it was what person or department of the CIA he reported to.

Because Kim Philby is a special case, I will use other examples to support my point. Nobody doubted that Kheiry Hammad was a spy; we thought he worked for Nasser. His flimsy cover, his nominal job as a correspondent for the Italian news agency Continentale, could not possibly have covered his huge bar expenses. Now, more and more evidence is beginning to suggest that he had a relationship with British Intelligence as well as with Nasser. In other words Hammad may have been a double agent; certainly his close relationship with Sefton Delmer and others connected with British Intelligence points in this direction. Although we now know much of what he did, it is still not possible to place him in terms of anyone's espionage hierarchy, which leaves the question of his real importance unanswered.

It is now common knowledge that British Intelligence sent Philby to the Middle East in the late fifties, after the defection of Burgess and MacLean cast doubt on his loyalty, leading to his investigation and clearance. He himself has admitted this, but not the claims that his allegiance was always to the KGB and Russia. The important question is whether British Intelligence knew about Kim's commitment to communism and sent him to the Middle East deliberately because they knew he was a Russian spy, or whether his masters were the naive people they are pictured to be.

The biggest Middle East political and journalistic story during Philby's six-year stay in Beirut was Iraq, which stood in the way of Nasser's attempt to control the area and create one big Arab country under his leadership. Both Russia and Britain supported an independent Iraq and were opposed to Nasser's ambitious plans to create a powerful Arab union because his success would have endangered their own interests in the region. This means that the British could have sent Philby to the area, afforded him a chance to help thwart Nasser and serve mutual Russian and British interests. But we do not know who, and what department, sent Philby to the Middle East. *The Economist* magazine, one of Philby's employers during his Beirut period, spoke of the foreign office asking them to hire him as Middle East correspondent in an editorial written after Philby's defection. Curiouser and curiouser.

Bill Eveland never hid his CIA parentage. But few in Beirut and the bar knew how important he was until another CIA agent, Miles Copeland, exposed Eveland's status in his book, *The Game of Nations*. The Copeland exposure, now verified, said that Eveland reported directly to the White House; he was a counterweight to the US ambassador to

Lebanon, Robert MacLintock. The simple need to have a counterweight to a local ambassador says a great deal about the Americans' confused and often contradictory policy in Lebanon and the Middle East, and confirms the oft-heard allegation that the CIA conducts its own foreign policy. Mostly, the CIA is out to punish those who disagree with America, while the State Department is out to convert them.

The case of barman Ali Bitar was simpler. He knew so much that one would have viewed his lack of any espionage connection as 'a wasted opportunity'. Because of his strong religious and nationalistic feeling, we suspected him of being another Nasser spy. He now admits having spied for Lebanese Security, but not everybody is convinced.

The one Yugoslav bicycle salesman who used the bar in the sixties was suspected of spying for his country. At that time, Yugoslavia's only export to the Middle East was bicycles, but the bar was an odd place to promote this trade. As a result, we accepted him as a spy who worked for Yugoslavia because no one else was foolish or inventive enough to concoct such a situation. Why not? After all, Syria's spies always carried worry beads and spoke with a distinct Damascene accent; given their inefficiency, they had a great deal to worry about.

Other spies used various means to hide their identity or purpose. British spy Anthony Cavendish found his love of food handy. He had the grill room name a soup after him and was known to consume fourteen lamb chops for lunch. People busied themselves with the obvious and there is little to tell about Anthony's successful espionage work.

As with Eveland, the question regarding visiting spies concerned the reason for their presence. Maurice Oldfield of MI6 came to the St George and to the bar, but we do not know why. The identities of senior CIA operatives Kim and Archie Roosevelt and of Nasser aide Mohammed Hasanein Heikal were known to everybody, but we never knew why they were there. The heads of Syrian, Egyptian, Turkish, Iraqi, Jordanian and Iranian intelligence services made occasional visits to the bar and more often than not their positions became known, though not their purpose.

So, the bar was full of spies – resident spies, visiting spies, Lebanese, Egyptian, British, American, Yugoslav and, undoubtedly, Russian spies. I personally know every spy discussed in this chapter and so, among other things, my judgement is highly subjective. There are many reasons why Kim Philby should head the list of bar spies. Not only was he the most famous among them, but his was an amazing career which continues to baffle and intrigue us. Much about this man and his activities remains unknown and is likely to stay that way. The one story all bar regulars remember about Kim Philby is how he married his third wife, Eleanor.

Eleanor had been married to Sam Pope Brewer of the *New York Times* and she had her own peripheral connection with the world of espionage. She had worked for George Britt, an OSS (the CIA's precursor) operative in Turkey after the Second World War. When she met Kim in 1958 her marriage to Sam was in bad shape and she fell for the boyish, handsome Brit. Their affair was a secret until the most famous marriage announcement in the history of the bar was made.

Brewer was standing at the bar by himself when, much to his surprise, Eleanor and Kim entered together and occupied a table on the terrace, just outside. Brewer reluctantly consented to join them only after Eleanor's fourth or fifth invitation. Eleanor then turned to Kim and said, 'Darling, tell him.' This, too, she repeated several times and then, despairing, she said, 'Kim and I . . .' She was interrupted by Kim, who stuttered, 'We, We, We would like to get married.' Sam hesitated before responding, 'I hope I am not in the way.' He returned to the bar and bought everybody a drink, but days later he went into a deep funk; friends said he realized that his only daughter Anne would have to live with the Philbys and his CIA friends told him that Kim was still suspected of being a Russian agent. Years later, little Anne became the centre of a complicated custody case which reached the US Supreme Court and which Sam won.

As Eleanor was more fond of the bar than Kim had been, they began to frequent it more than ever before, though, unlike other regulars, Kim continued to frequent other places, particularly the Normandy Hotel. Like the proverbial spy, Kim drank a lot; his daytime visits to the bar usually followed stops at other drinking spots. But Kim's celebrated ability to hold his drink is a myth, probably the exaggeration of writers wishing to add colour to his already colourful life. He had a regular drinker's tolerance for alcohol, but no more. He often drank himself into a stupor and on a good number of occasions he had to be helped out of the bar. Ali Bitar, who should know, supports my contention, as do my father and Lebanese journalist Hanna Ghossun.

Kim always looked slightly dishevelled, an attractive man of letters in a sports jacket and corduroy trousers that had seen better days. His stammer and his tendency to speak in a soft, gravelly voice gave an impression of shyness. Together with his longer-than-average hair, a middle-age slouch and a naughty twinkle, they all added to his physical attractiveness. Women liked Kim and he returned the compliment. One might have called him a natural flirt; his very being carried a sexual suggestiveness.

My own recollections of Philby produce three stories which are very much worth re-telling. Eleanor had liked me; which meant she paid attention to me as a junior member of the bar press when we sat in drinking circles with older, more important people present. One day in 1959 when we made up such a group, she leaned towards me and said, 'Saïd, do you know what Kim calls the White House now? . . . the tomb of the well-known soldier.' We both laughed at the expense of poor Eisenhower and she leaned towards Kim and said, 'Darling, Saïd likes your joke.'

On another occasion, most of the bar press were at Dick Kallsen's of CBS for cocktails. Kim had plainly had too much; at one point he was pestering Nicole Streithorst (Tom's wife), trying to fondle her and eventually even unzipping his trousers. Tom, rightly annoyed, came close to punching Kim in the mouth and would have done so but for my intervention. Kim's appreciation of my peace-making efforts made him unusually friendly. He put his arm around my shoulder, muttering, 'We messed it up, but you're young – do something about it.'

A third recollection of Philby is a story which he told a drinking circle at the bar. It goes like this: a missionary spends twenty years in Africa, after which he manages to convert one black native to Christian ways. The night after the missionary's crowning achievement, the black enters his tent to alert him to the presence of a hungry animal, a tiger, around the mission station. The missionary looks at his convert and is suddenly full of fear – not of the tiger, but of the convert. He reaches for his rifle and shoots the convert dead. The following day he starts working to convert another black.

I asked Ralph Izzard, who was one of the listeners to this particular Philby story, what it and other Philby stories meant. Ralph, who was as close to Kim as anyone in Beirut, refused to elaborate on the stories, but instead gave me a refreshing insight into how Philby handled the after-effects of drinking. He apparently followed what might be called the Kim Philby Hangover Cure. It had nothing to do with special drink or food; it was purely psychological. Kim refused to think about the hangover and instead occupied himself by doing something 'positive': telephoning old girlfriends, paying bills or going for a walk in a smelly *souk*. These all sound highly questionable 'positives' to me.

The one aspect of Philby's spy life which I can report with authority is the amount of American, CIA, hounding to which he was subjected until his defection. When CIA agent James Russell Barracks tried to hire me to monitor Philby, he told me that the Americans were keen to determine whether 'a relationship' existed between Kim and one of the bar's waiters, an Armenian with known leftist tendencies named Haig. I rejected Barracks' generous offer because I liked Kim and Haig and found the whole thing distasteful.

Using subtler tactics, John Fistere, King Hussein's CIA-appointed public relations aide, went out of his way to befriend Kim and Eleanor, both in the bar and outside it. A former OSS officer and *Time* business executive, full of Madison-Avenue pleasantness, Fistere had very little in common with the Philbys but often drank with them at the bar and invited them to his frequent cocktail parties. Fistere went further; he hired Kim's pretty daughter Josephine to work for him at a time when her main interest in life seemed to be her teenage crush on her boy friend, my younger brother Afif. A trained, Arabic-speaking Lebanese girl would have done a better job than the inexperienced, eighteen-year-old Philby girl.

That Fistere had a professional interest in Philby the spy is beyond doubt; friends of Philby, who prefer to remain anonymous, confirm this. Nine of those I interviewed, all honourable people who take considerable care about what they say and some of them sophisticated spy-watchers, explicitly accused Fistere of heading a cabal to get Philby. Two went so far as to insist that Fistere's efforts and the American determination to trap Philby had as much as anything or anyone to do with his defection.

Another CIA agent who knew Kim Philby well was Miles Copeland. Miles' interest in the spy continued after his defection; he wrote Philby a letter about making fools of everybody because all had thought that Kim was strictly a British agent. In fairness, Copeland was not a bar regular, but his odd appearance there was always accompanied by so much commotion that *Time* correspondent Wilton Wynn pronounced an unforgettable accolade: 'Miles is the only man who ever used the CIA for cover.' Copeland continues to describe Kim as 'a dear friend of mine', though Philby declined to return the compliment in his book, *My Secret War*.

Edward R. F. Sheehan, a celebrated freelance American journalist, arrived in Beirut a few months after the Philby defection to investigate one of the more intriguing espionage episodes of all time. The result of his meticulous research and literally dozens of interviews was a long, well-written article in the *Saturday Evening Post* which contained a number of highly questionable statements. Sheehan, a totally honourable journalist, admitted to me a year after publication and a small argument that thirty per cent of the article was untrue; he claimed that he had been 'misled' and regretted the fact. One of the people with whom Sheehan spent a great deal of time when in Beirut writing the article was Miles Copeland.

More curious than Sheehan's admission was the inclusion of his story in *An Anthology of Great Spy Stories*, a collection edited by Allen Dulles, former head of the CIA. It is safe to assume that Dulles knew the facts as well, if not better, than Sheehan did. Why did Dulles choose to promote his highly questionable version of the Philby defection? Was there something in the story that the CIA – or part of it – wanted to advance? Did the story originate with Miles Copeland or another CIA hand? If spying was a simple business I would say that Dulles, like me, enjoyed the overall presentation.

American interest in Philby manifested itself in many ways: Barracks openly wanted him watched, Fistere extended the rules of the game to the point of hiring Philby's daughter and Miles Copeland, by his own admission a major CIA operative during the Philby years in Beirut, maintained a curious friendship. But it didn't stop there; Molly Izzard, wife of Ralph and an author in her own right, gives innumerable examples of late-night telephone calls to their place every time Kim stayed with them. The callers were always 'drunken American ladies' who were checking on Kim's whereabouts. This degree of American attention to Philby amounted to merciless hounding. Miles Copeland himself attests to this in his book, *The Game of Nations*, and suggests that a great many people, British as well as American, were involved.

The British Philby-monitoring operation was much more subtle; it certainly didn't show its colours around the bar. However one felt about Kim, there was something beyond the naive in the American moves against him. Most were downright stupid, winning him the sympathy of a number of bar regulars, including some British journalists. Eventually, the belief in Kim's guilt or innocence practically divided along national lines, with the Americans believing he was guilty and the British defending him.

Shortly before he died in Moscow, Kim Philby told Philip

Knightley of the *Sunday Times* that British Intelligence had allowed him to defect rather than face the consequences of putting him on trial, with the inevitable damage to the whole espionage establishment and to many of its senior members. It would have been easy to get Kim in Beirut, to arrest him and bundle him back to London as diplomatic luggage. But did the Americans opt for the same thing, allowing Kim to defect, or did Philby just slip through the net? The latter is the more plausible explanation because, one month after the Philby defection, one of the Americans in charge of monitoring him was unceremoniously fired from his job.

Another extraordinary aspect of Philby's character was demonstrated in Beirut and the bar. Once, in 1958, a local photographer was passing around the bar pictures of mutilated bodies killed in a bomb explosion during communal disturbances. Unlike the rest of us present, Kim had a difficult time looking at the gory pictures. This incident was in line with other stories about his behaviour, his objection to his father's using live scorpions to teach his grandchildren about the natural sciences or the report of his fainting when one child cut his leg badly. This picture of squeamishness does not fit the image of the super-spy who sent dozens of Western agents to certain death and personally supervised the undoing of a Russian agent in Turkey when the latter wanted to defect to the West.

Lastly, there is the question of Kim's complex relationship with his famous Orientalist father, St John Philby. Much has been made of Kim's love for his father, to the extent of attributing his espousal of communism to the humiliation of his father by the British Foreign Office, which did not appreciate the elder Philby's achievement in helping to create Saudi Arabia. To me, Kim's attitude towards his father is no different from that of most English public school boys. If anything, there was considerable ambiguity in the relationship because the elder Philby, who had converted to Islam, had tried to apply the religion's strict rules to the behaviour of Kim and his sister when they were young. Philby *père* once slapped his daughter for not behaving like a good Moslem girl; Kim resented the incident and remembered it.

Besides drink, the one aspect of Philby's character which agrees with what has been reported in innumerable books and articles is his appeal to women. One time his father, who was well aware of this trait in his son's character, observed an attractive American woman hovering around Kim and said, 'Poor Kim – he's in trouble again.' A young girlfriend of mine visiting Beirut from California saw him walk into the bar and could not take her eyes off him. She described him as 'a manly teddy bear'.

Kim had a difficult time saying no to women and I have no doubt that some of the women who went to bed with him had hopes of a Mata Hari conclusion to things; they did it to debrief him. I know one lady, an occasional bar visitor and a CIA plant, who still refers to her liaison with Kim with pride, but she has refused to go 'on the record' with her recollections.

The most intriguing part of Kim's open life in Beirut was the CIA's relentless effort to 'neutralize' him by keeping him under constant surveillance. His drinking, womanizing and squeamishness had been with him before. Both the Russians and MI6 had accepted these elements in his character, though normally they would have brought to an end the career of a lesser spy.

Whereas Kim's Beirut life is easy to retrace, his disappearance and its consequences are the opposite. Why did MI5 and the CIA fail to examine mail addressed to him at the Normandy Hotel? For months after his defection the concierge at the Normandy solicited help in 'what to do about Mr Kim's post'. The behaviour of Lebanese Security was even more intriguing: deputy chief Omar Nueiri first showed my father and *Time*'s Bill McHale a pass issued in the name of one 'Heroold Philiby' allowing him to board a Russian ship in Beirut's harbour. The *Time* team were allowed to examine what appeared to be a genuine document twice before it disappeared. At first, Nueiri claimed it was a fake; then he changed his mind and, to the amazement of

Abu Saïd and McHale, insisted that they, Lebanese Security, knew nothing of Pheelby, Philiby or whatever his name was. Coupled with the oft-neglected fact that there were no repercussions to Kim's defection – no one else was uncovered, even interrogated – the inevitable conclusion must be that his defection was facilitated and that whoever accommodated him wanted the whole thing hushed up and forgotten.

Two months before he died, I asked four people who were close to Kim in Beirut the same question: would they be surprised if Kim one day re-surfaced in the West? They had said 'no' and I had agreed with them. Now we will never know.

7

SPIES AND FRIENDS
– THE CIA AND OTHERS

If Kim Philby was the perfect picture of the mysterious, quiet, retiring bar spy, then the little-known but extremely effective James Russell Barracks was the opposite; loud, brash and old-womanish. Jim Barracks is probably the most underrated spy to operate out of Beirut and the bar in the fifties and sixties. His lack of notoriety is due in part to the fact that he died in the sixties and, unlike fellow CIA operatives Copeland and Eveland, he had no chance to write his memoirs. Most people did not like Barracks and tended to dismiss him as a lightweight, an attitude which persisted after his death. Even former colleagues who know better refuse to speak of his achievements lest they detract from their own; he has no advocates.

Born on a farm near Urbana, Illinois, and educated at Yale University, Barracks made little effort to hide either his CIA identity or his homosexuality. Either label would have been enough to limit his usefulness, particularly at that time, but an uncanny ability to get close to people and situations which mattered overcame both hurdles. His open, firm belief that the end justified the means and his inherent bitchiness did, along with other personal traits, set him apart from the gentleman spies of the bar, Kim Philby, John Fistere and Archie Roosevelt.

Barracks tended to be over-effusive: he always greeted people as long-lost friends and took time out, in an Arab way, to enquire about their health and families, even when the subjects of such solicitous enquiries didn't like them. This facet of his character got out of hand in the presence of important people; his weakness showed in an unbecoming insistence on calling them by their first names, clasping their hand in both of his and patting them on the back.

Though his CIA work was obvious, Barracks still went through the pretence of having a cover. He pretended to represent American companies wishing to trade with the Middle East and the list of companies he represented included some major defence contractors. The profusion of calling cards to support this image and endless bar meetings to discuss commerce stopped short of producing even one business deal. I could not trace a single one.

That someone so obvious and with so many strikes against him could operate effectively within the espionage establishment is an excellent example of the power of Western intelligence institutions, particularly of the CIA, in developing countries. Instead of deterring people from dealing with him, Barracks' weaknesses were usable assets, making him extra recognizable to anyone who wished to cooperate with the CIA. There were a lot of people with this desire in Beirut and in the bar. A somewhat envious British MI6 agent observed: 'Nothing came out badly for people who have an organization as powerful as the CIA behind them. They won in spite of themselves.'

The Lebanese presidential hopeful was a case in point. Having decided that CIA support was a prerequisite for election as president of Lebanon, this man sought CIA backing through Barracks, who strung him along. The two became an inseparable bar duo and their appearances together there served the purposes of the Lebanese, who wanted to advertise his American connection. On the other hand, Barracks had nothing to lose: he learned about the machinations of Lebanese presidential politics and used the new-found relationship to pressure the leading candidate into a friendlier posture towards the US. Nothing was lost when this man failed to win; on the contrary, he maintained his relationship with the CIA because he had already compromised himself.

Barracks' real identity also served his purpose in the case of Iraq. The 1958 anti-monarchist revolution in that country left it with a pro-Russian, anti-Western government. Many

Iraqi politicians and businessmen unhappy with this turn of events fled to Beirut, eventually forming a club within a club at the bar, where they advocated the overthrow of the leftist government and its replacement by one friendlier to the West.

For the bar Iraqi group, cooperating with Barracks was a natural thing to do; after all, he was the CIA. They met him at the bar on a regular basis and, through their contacts back in Iraq, provided him with information about conditions there. Iraqi exiles hoped that the US would act on their information and topple their common enemy. The US never delivered, but Barracks' meticulous manipulations kept the flow of information going for a long time.

Barracks' biggest recruitment coup, and he had a few, was the enlistment of the deputy secretary general of the League of Arab States to work for the CIA. The person in question was Lebanese, an intelligent, able man with an intellectual commitment to capitalism; he was a staunch anti-communist. In the fifties and sixties the League of Arab States, whose primary aim was the development of a common policy for the Arab countries, was dominated by President Nasser of Egypt. Towering over his contemporary Arab leaders and popular with the masses, Nasser had reduced the League to a mouthpiece for his socialist, anti-Western and somewhat pro-Russian policies. The deputy secretary was opposed to Nasser's policies and determined to undermine him.

The deputy secretary's son-in-law, a well-known Lebanese newspaper editor, answered his call for help and arranged for him to meet Barracks, the local lighthouse for people wishing to find an American connection. Dispensing with his initial misgivings, the deputy secretary met Barracks at the bar to confirm their obvious mutual interest.

Barracks acted as the deputy secretary's case officer; first, he debriefed him in his own department over a period of two days. Later, after the Lebanese turncoat returned to Cairo to resume his duties, he organized an uninterrupted flow of information through a number of messengers who came to the bar on a regular basis, particularly soon after Arab League meetings. Though an idealogue spy is often worthy of respect – definitely in a different class from the mercenary spy – I have always wondered how much damage was done to the League of Arab States by the Lebanese renegade.

Barracks' obviousness was an advantage, but I am still at a loss as to why his hounding of Philby was so open, why he insisted on dragging the presidential hopeful and deputy secretary to the bar and why the CIA allowed these things to happen. They even included a present PLO leader who was 'retained' by Barracks during the fifties and sixties. Brigadier-General Radi Abdallah of Jordan was the Arab counterpart of James Barracks; he, too, wanted to be noticed and known. The one-time military aide-de-camp to King Hussein and Jordanian Minister of the Interior typified the third-world intelligence officer, even in his use of dark glasses. Radi began using the bar in the mid-fifties. Then a colonel, he was Jordan's military attaché in Beirut at a time when Nasser was trying to undermine King Hussein and his pro-Western government. His success in using the bar at that time left such a deep impression on him that he continued to use it after his promotions, commuting from Amman solely for that purpose.

As Hussein's chief military aide-de-camp and Minister of Interior, his functions were one and the same: to foil the plots of anti-Hussein, pro-Nasser Jordanians, to cooperate with Arab and foreign intelligence services opposed to Nasser and to deflect the latter's threat of regional domination. He reported directly to Hussein and the Nasser threat was real, so one could say that the fate of the country was in his hands. Radi Abdallah was an able, effective intelligence officer but, unlike Barracks, his weaknesses were not his strength: he suffered from maladies which appear to afflict third-world security and army officers, a vulnerability to women and money.

Radi was a man of considerable charm, a handsome six-footer with an imposing physique and ruddy complexion who added to his natural magnetism by being extremely polite, by dressing in an elegant, sober manner and by judicial use of a ready, biting sense of humour. He stood out in every way.

To monitor the constant plotting of anti-Hussein Jordanians who used the bar as a base, Radi relied on traditional methods laced with personal invention. His informers were the usual lot of taxi drivers, bartenders, hotel clerks, cabaret girls and Lebanese journalists. Because his government was poor he seldom paid them enough for their efforts and his lack of funds was exacerbated by the use of whatever money was available to him for 'personal reasons'. To compensate for this serious shortcoming, Radi occasionally blackmailed people into continued cooperation after he stopped paying them and, in other cases, he promised money but did not pay because the information was not 'worth it'.

Radi was more a cinematic cloak-and-dagger type than the other spies, more like the members of South American army juntas that we see on television than like Western intelligence operatives. His dark glasses were part of a bigger picture which included gold rings, contradictory alibis for his movements and short, sharp sentences which added to the mystery – 'I am hunting a dog'. He enjoyed his work, and it showed.

In liaising with other intelligence services, Radi haughtily and rightly refused to deal with lowly functionaries. Instead he dealt with the chiefs: in the case of the Lebanese, directly with President Chamoun and in the case of the CIA, he once refused to talk to Barracks' Lebanese sidekick. Though he worked with them very closely, Radi viewed bar CIA operatives and the CIA with considerable misgivings. He always assumed that the mutual interest which bound them had built-in limitations because the Americans were 'capable of doing a hundred and eighty degree turn for intellectual reasons which don't make sense to normal people'. On the other hand, though his British training made him favour them, we know little except that he was in direct touch with Maurice Oldfield, the former head of MI6, and that the two did meet in Beirut.

The ruthlessness which typifies third-world security officers was part of Radi's character. In his case, it derived from a strong belief that Arabs are incapable of ideological commitment and that traditional rulers like Hussein would thus prevail and the Nassers of this world would lose. This created in him a genuine hate for the forces of change in the Middle East.

Radi Abdallah's weaknesses were also deep-rooted. His humble bedouin background left him with an insatiable appetite for cocktail parties and casinos, and for the women and gambling which went with them. His appeal to women and his generosity to them got him into trouble, unfortunate affairs with the wives of foreign correspondents and diplomats accompanied by presents of gold bracelets and diamond pins which eventually compromised him. His gambling worsened over time and, along with a hefty jewellery shop account, became his undoing. His career ended in 1972.

None of this should detract from Radi's intelligence and success. He stood by Hussein through turbulent times, in the process unmasking several plots against the king, feats which earned him the grudging respect of Western colleagues. He was a self-educated man who rose to the top through hard work and cunning. He fell victim to weaknesses which afflict the hatchet men of dictators – his loneliness and his inflated picture of his indispensability made him careless and hence of no use to Hussein. Hussein sacrificed him the moment Radi's liabilities exceeded his contribution, but, aware of what lay behind Radi's initial success, Hussein told his replacement to keep an eye on the bar.

Unlike Radi, Kheiry Hammad was an intellectual idealogue spy, his spying an extension of philosophical commitment. One of the most regular of the bar habitués, Kheiry was a firm believer in Nasser's ambitions to unite the Arabs and realize Palestinian Arab dreams to defeat Israel. A fat, ungainly man who used the Continentale news agency for cover, Hammad combined the largesse of establishment Arabs with a sophisticated worldliness which embraced a love of books, wine and food. His character overcame the unattractiveness of his obesity; he was the most attractive ugly man I've ever known.

Kheiry's main known activity was recruiting kindred spirits, other believers in Arab dreams, to spy for Nasser. So many bar and Beirut people then belonged to this group that he had an easy job. Despite the high number of volunteers, he was still faced with the problems of authenticating information and establishing on-going rather than occasional sources. Because his foreign correspondent's cover facilitated his movements, Kheiry was able to establish contact with suspicious people without adverse consequences. He focussed on Lebanese journalists, waiters with leftist tendencies, radical student leaders, exiles from Arab countries opposed to Nasser and mysterious characters who appeared and disappeared without leaving a trace. Many of Hammad's contacts came to the bar, some even worked there, and it was the place which witnessed his unique style.

I can vouch for Hammad's recruitment operation because I was subjected to it; he made me an offer to work with him. His approach was low-key, an appeal to the ever-present anti-Israeli feelings of the listener; he made it extremely difficult for me to turn him down. He tried to transform the notion of rejecting Israel into a more concrete posture, a contribution towards its defeat. There was no promise of money, just glory; the honour of service was supposed to be enough. To him, people who did this type of thing for money were a lower species.

Because he approached potential recruits with meticulous care after long observation, Hammad had a high record of success. When he succeeded, Hammad proceeded to endow his operatives with a sense of importance; they were on a psyschological high which made them work hard and eliminated the chances of discontinuing their services. One of the waiters in the bar and in the grill room worked for Hammad. Palestinian activists wishing to give expression to their frustration came to see him in the bar and PTT clerks, who in pre-telex days were privy to the contents of correspondents' cablegrams, divulged their secrets. There were also taxi drivers and two Moslem members of the Lebanese security service.

Hammad's success is best measured by the efforts of the CIA and others to turn him and make him work for them.

Though always short of funds, with a limited budget over-taxed by love of food and wine, Hammad appears to have resisted their generous offers. Eventually food and drink ruined his health and he died of over-indulgence. We know little about his achievements beyond his recruiting successes.

Philby, Barracks, Abdallah and Hammad each represented a specific school of espionage, a method of operation. John Fistere was another type of spy, one whose nominal job had a covert side, a situation where the cover and the real job are one and the same, but where aspects of the covert activity go beyond the overt one.

Fistere's nominal job was public relations work for King Hussein from headquarters in Beirut. His covert job was to promote the king in a way consistent with US foreign policy objectives in the Middle East. His loyalty was to the CIA. A former OSS officer in the Middle East during the Second World War, Fistere had excellent credentials in the public relations field through a long career at *Time*. He returned to the Middle East to promote His Majesty after the CIA decided the latter needed help and Fistere's background was perfect for the job. He was a well-qualified propagandist.

His overt activities, the nominal job of working with the foreign press corps and the business community, he performed quite well, mostly at the bar. He planted a number of pro-Hussein stories, killed unfavourable ones and attracted a few foreign businesses to Jordan.

Fistere's downfall came when he got involved in matters for which he was not prepared. He once wrote a speech for Hussein which was delivered at the UN. In trying to promote US policy through Hussein, Fistere included a scathing attack on Nasser which exceeded political helpfulness; certainly it was unacceptable to the Arab mind and culture. Even the most anti-Nasser of Hussein's Arab advisers and members of his cabinet cringed at Fistere's language and thought that the speech did Hussein more harm than good. But it was not the only time when a conflict of loyalties arose between Fistere's nominal job and his real job.

The situation of Commander Robert Hutchison, USNR,

director general of American Friends of the Middle East (AFME) in the fifties and sixties, was similar to Fistere's. His nominal job, the supervision of a humanitarian organization committed to improving the image of America among the Arab people, was also his CIA job, a covert attempt at creating an image of a friendly, benevolent America. Hutchison was another propagandist.

AFME translated American literary works into Arabic, secured scholarships at American universities for needy Arab students and promoted goodwill trips between the US and Arab countries. Basically, AFME promoted everything American without suffering from the stigma of official efforts which were subject to suspicion and rejection. The AFME people, to render themselves more effective, were outspoken critics of Israel, something not possible for people operating in an overt official capacity, the diplomats.

Commander Hutchison and his deputy, Charles Hulac, were bar regulars whenever they were in Beirut, always dispensing human interest stories about the good reception given to bits of Americana by the Arabs and complaining about the influence of the Jewish lobby on US foreign policy. They always spoke of things being better when the Arabs knew 'the true feelings of the Americans', as if that mattered more than the official policy of the US. AFME activities were a highly legitimate extension of intelligence work, an attempt to dilute the negative effects of an unfriendly foreign policy. The Hutchison-Hulac efforts may be questioned because not even the simplest scholarship-winning Arab fell victim to their propaganda, but there is no denying that they lived up to their brief and avoided meddling.

These examples of bar spies and spying represent a tiny sample of what happens in the wider world of espionage. Even in terms of bar activities, they are no more than a small fraction of what happened. Much remains unknown. What did Maurice Oldfield of MI6 and Richard Helms, former director of the CIA, do when they were there? And very little is known, for example, about the activities of CIA cousins

Kim and Archie Roosevelt or the various British operatives who used journalism for cover.

There is considerable diversity in spying: the aim of the spy, the cover he uses and how the spy behaves. Other than drinking a lot, Philby, Abdallah, Hammad, Fistere and Hutchison had very little in common. Their attitude to each other at the bar betrayed an implicit sense of camaraderie, a silent admiration for each other. But, as we will see, politeness was skin deep when it stood in the way of achievement.

8

IT'S A DIRTY GAME,
IT'S A DEADLY GAME

Kim Philby was not the only bar spy whose meek outward behaviour concealed a killer. Beneath the clubby atmosphere enveloping the bar were the hard professionals, people totally committed to success regardless of cost to others.

The activities of this group were often stranger than the shenanigans of their fictional counterparts – with one basic difference. In real life, using dirty tricks is neither as easy, spontaneous or romantic as James Bond makes it seem; instead they are practised as a last resort, though, as in fiction, they can often result in death or the destruction of lives. Most spies are too deliberate to indulge in individual acts of violence.

Let us take the case of Abdul Aziz Muamar, one-time adviser to King Saud of Saudi Arabia and a frequent visitor to the bar and its terrace during the fifties and sixties. He was a rare creature; in addition to his position of power, he was highly educated, cosmopolitan, polite in an endearing, old-fashioned Arab way and, despite all surrounding pressures which reeked of corruption, he was clean.

A believer in evolutionary change incorporating traditional values, he was aware of the sick atmosphere consuming the Saudi royal court and tried his best to contain it. Muamar's way was to set an example of honesty and then methodically, energetically work against the more corrupt members of the king's entourage. He became a resented outsider – which didn't please him – but because he had nothing to hide, he felt he had nothing to fear.

When in Beirut, Muamar used the bar to visit with foreign correspondents, businessmen and occasionally spies; to get a feel for international affairs affecting his country and the

Middle East; and to do a better job for His Majesty and the Saudi government. What he heard and what he knew propelled him toward open advocacy of change and of the need to reform the court from within. He did not believe that replacing the royal family was possible or desirable because of the country's state of development, though he feared the consequences of the unchecked behaviour of its members.

By 1964 Muamar's views had become known to King Faisal, who had just replaced his corrupt brother with a mandate for change. These views were known to a number of the bar press, who admired Muamar, and eventually to members of the bar CIA, who were historically less tolerant and who viewed Muamar's opinions with considerable disquiet. They equated advocacy of change, even when aimed at containing corruption, with subversion. To them, Muamar was dangerous because he proposed to rock the boat while Faisal was steering ever so cautiously and conservatively. Moreover, an advocate of change was also undoubtedly anti-American; he threatened those American interests which supported the royal family in order to maintain oil interests in Saudi Arabia. Muamar became a designated CIA target; he had to be neutralized.

Without betraying their purpose, the bar CIA unofficially debriefed every journalist who had ever spoken to Muamar or knew something about him. They offered money to bar staff to obtain information against him. They unsuccessfully chased Muamar around Beirut, looking for possible weaknesses – drinking, womanizing or gambling – and they went out of their way to establish his connection to Nasser, then the arch-enemy of the Saudi royal family.

Finally, though he was neither a flawed man nor a Nasser follower, a huge damning report was prepared by the bar CIA for the CIA station chief in Saudi Arabia, who made sure King Faisal read it. Early in 1965 Muamar was arrested upon return to Saudi Arabia and sent to an undisclosed jail. The few subscribers to Muamar's ideas vanished in thin air; expediency came ahead of principle. The news of his arrest hit the bar like a storm; an angry journalist, realizing that he had been duped, called a CIA man 'a pimp's pimp' and a waiter who had praised Muamar to the Americans sighed in despair and said, 'What the hell do the Americans want, ignorant people?'

But there was nothing to be done. Muamar was never charged with any crime, let alone tried. But for seven long years his family and others who admired his undoubted honesty had no idea whether he was dead or alive – he simply vanished. Only after his sad, broken wife personally appealed to the king for information about his location was Muamar released.

He emerged from prison a blind, shattered man, his mind all but gone, a distant shadow of the sprightly, articulate man he had once been. Saudi Arabia and decency are the less for his 'neutralization'. The CIA agent who engineered Muamar's downfall continued to drink at the bar as if nothing had happened, happy in the knowledge that Saudi Arabia was safe for the West – and very corrupt.

Far removed from the bar, and lacking any connection with his brother's affairs, Colonel Saud Muamar, Abdul Aziz's brother, an-up-and-coming officer of the Saudi army – my dear friend and one-time school roommate – was arrested by the same king in 1968 during a purge of suspect elements from the armed forces. Because his name was Muamar, he was judged guilty without proof and tortured to death. I do not usually remember dreams, but for fifteen years after Saud's death, I suffered a recurring nightmare in which my lost, much-missed friend pleads with me to 'do something to help us, Said, do something to help us'. The dream ceased only after I made a promise to try.

The savagery of the bar CIA was not confined to non-Americans. They were intolerant even of fellow Americans who stood in the way of their unholy mission, as proved the case with a correspondent for an important news weekly who, through conviction, opposed some CIA and US government policies, and was bold enough to express his doubts in his reports.

For the longest time, the bar CIA worked on the man directly, trying to change his point of view. When this did not work, they tried to put pressure on his employer, but the magazine supported its man, expressing total confidence in his professional judgement. Then one of the bar CIA decided to attack the correspondent 'where it hurt': through his bed-hopping wife.

Initially the correspondent's wife, an unknowing accomplice, came to the bar with her CIA bait while her husband was out of town on an assignment. The raised eyebrows had more to do with her lack of tact than with her known vulnerability and no one suspected the real motive. This performance repeated itself and the ungallant seducer kept parading his prey at the bar. As if this were not ugly enough, the news was transmitted to the correspondent's employer, with a suggestion that he be transferred.

Eventually, somehow, the husband found out. But he was not embarrassed into absenting himself from the bar, turning silent or shamefully leaving Beirut altogether. He became extremely angry and even more vocal in his condemnation of the CIA. His wife survived the ordeal, though the couple later divorced. In the end, the CIA paid the price. The correspondent's hatred of the agency became legendary and he did them disservice in several parts of the world where he later served.

Nor was the incident involving the correspondent's wife the only CIA 'operation' which went wrong. One major blunder could almost have come from the elegant pen of John Le Carré, a bizarre episode whose causes are darker than simple miscalculation.

The young man who came to the bar in 1959 was tall, handsome and full of the graces of a more mature man. His Southern drawl was pronounced and was accompanied by gallantry to women, a relaxed, courtly way of addressing waiters and an undisguised interest in the bar.

But why was he there? What was the twenty-four-year-old North Carolinian grandson of a former vice president of the United States doing in the bar? He said he was escaping an estranged wife who didn't want to give him a divorce. Lo and behold, his wife arrived as if on cue, along with two poodles, stayed at the St George for a week and then departed. By then he had come to know and like the bar crowd and had decided to stay. He wasn't in a hurry to find a job.

Though the bar regulars were a suspicious lot, stranger tales had been told: they took the young man to their hearts. He seemed to be enjoying himself, if spending time and money in a posh place are anything to go by. Soon the young man was seen constantly in the company of a known CIA operative, which revived the bar regulars' suspicions. No one could figure out how they had met and the difference in their ages made them an odd, contradictory twosome.

Now we all decided that our young friend was a CIA man, not only because of the company he kept, but because he suddenly possessed greater knowledge of politics than was justified by his mere two-month stay. He unexpectedly began consorting with Lebanese politicians and newspaper editors and other CIA types. But he seemed a bit too young and effete to be an important CIA operative.

Six months passed with nothing to report about our young Southern gentleman. Then, suddenly, he appeared in the company of a Swiss, the head of a major international organization. Something was finally happening, we told ourselves, because the CIA had already tried, without success, to determine whether the Swiss in question was a Russian KGB agent. More experienced hands had failed to undo the slippery Swiss, so what was the wisdom behind surrendering his case to a novice? Our reflections came to an end three months later; the young American disappeared as suddenly as he appeared and neither his CIA mentor nor Swiss friend would say anything except that he had gone back to America.

But the matter didn't rest there; the mystery of his disappearance was deepened by the appearance at the bar of Omar Nueiri, deputy chief of security in Beirut. Nueiri was open on two points: the young American had been deported on twenty-four-hour notice and, as implied by his presence, Lebanese security wanted to know more about him.

It was my luck to run into the mysterious American in 1968 in the Wednesday Club in New York city. I recognized the still-young man sitting alone with a girl in a secluded corner and decided to approach him. I got more than I bargained for. He introduced me to his wife and asked me to join them. Soon he reached into his jacket and, in a most bizarre twist, produced his old passport and pictures of himself with various Lebanese personalities. Obviously drunk, he begged me to tell his wife who the people were, to convince her that he had once been involved 'in important things'. I obliged as best I could, but made a point of having lunch with him a few days later.

Our first lunch produced nothing. It took two months and many lunches, all of which I paid for because he, a clerk with the city of New York, was scarcely able to support his wife and young daughter, and he finally came through with the full story.

He admitted to having been a CIA man, or boy. He had been sent to Beirut to do a specific job, to trap the Swiss suspect. The only thing certain about his target was his homosexuality. The handsome Southerner was supposed to 'get close to him', and he had succeeded. They had become very friendly and he thought he was to be promoted because the Swiss was indeed a Russian spy. What torpedoed his plans was most unexpected: his CIA case officer in Beirut, another homosexual, had fallen in love with him. The closer he got to his target, the more jealous his case officer had become. But the reason for his deportation from Lebanon and dismissal from the CIA were a mystery. No one had told him anything. They didn't have to.

Eight months later, when I visited Beirut, I called on Nueiri to tell him about my discovery so he might tell me more. Nueiri only smiled broadly, following every statement of mine by 'Is that right?' Finally I asked how it fit with what he knew.

According to Nueiri, the Beirut CIA handed over a file on the young man purporting to show that he was crossing into Israel from Lebanon with his Swiss friend. The CIA requested that he be deported to avoid 'an incident', because crossing into Israel was illegal except for those, like the Swiss, whose work exempted them. Lebanese security obliged, but Nueiri had been curious: the CIA did not normally squeal on American citizens. The man who requested the deportation was the very man named by the New York city clerk as his case officer, the man who had fallen in love with him.

I have no hard evidence as to how the case officer manipulated this situation. The New York clerk had been told enough when he was fired to deduce that the CIA thought he was having an affair with the Swiss and feared that he would join his lover and become a Russian spy. But the man was not made from the stuff of double agents. He was a sad, pathetic figure, but so is an organization which would employ someone so manifestly weak.

Is it possible that a theory of 'alienation' can explain how people with twisted natures become spies. That would certainly seem to apply to the case of the top CIA agent operating under ethnic cover (he was Lebanese).

Unlike his friend Barracks, the Lebanese agent did everything to hide his homosexuality, even to the extent of marrying twice and fathering three boys. An occasional visitor to the bar, this man was opposed to everything Arab because he feared Moslem domination of the Middle East. That the Moslem Middle East accepted and lived in harmony with its Christians for centuries did not affect his thinking. This haughty, arrogant man laced his everyday conversation with acid anti-Arab comments and had a penchant for picking up taxi drivers who talked. His wife's affair with the late President Chamoun of Lebanon was the worst-kept secret in Beirut.

His sordid lifestyle aside, this man's politics favoured violence. During Nasser's time he continuously advocated a Western military expedition to topple the popular leader and others who did not espouse pro-Western policies. Later, he was responsible for arming extremist Christian elements within Lebanon and supported an all-out war to annihilate their Moslem countrymen. His evil advocacy of violence was directed at decision-makers within the CIA and the Christian community of Lebanon.

What was the aim of this man? I have followed his career from a safe distance for almost twenty years in hope of writing a book about him and cannot unearth a single instance where he directed his energies to something positive, say, the improvement of US-Arab relations or the peaceful settlement of Lebanon's sectarian problems. He had, and retains, a desire to destroy.

While our subject may have been effective in his information-gathering activity, I cannot but wonder about how the CIA viewed him. His commitment to anti-Arab, anti-Moslem movements and people implies that the CIA itself held the same views, something which is contrary to the State Department's policy, which favours friendly relations with Arabs and Moslems.

This is yet another example of the CIA's perverted ways. They relied on the vulgarity of Barracks, used the weakness of the Southern gentleman until it backfired, allowing a senior agent to hound a junior one in the process, and accepted, perhaps encouraged, the hatred of their ethnic agent for his own people. Is the CIA capable of attracting normal committed people? The alienation theory is well worth considering – in another book.

Until the recent exposures of the Pollard and Walker cases, the Americans viewed British Intelligence with unjustified smugness. They believed that American agents, unlike their British counterparts, did not betray their country the way Philby, Blake, Burgess, MacLean and Blunt did. Not only has time proved this assertion wrong, but also American Intelligence suffers from its own weaknesses.

To illustrate what happens to some old CIA hands who leave under a cloud when they are fired for reasons which are seldom explained, I relate the following secondhand account, which was told to me by someone who, for reasons which will become obvious, would rather that he and the subject of the story remain anonymous.

'I knew the guy . . . he was a bar fixture for many years.

. . . Everybody knew what he did because, like a lot of the CIA boys, he didn't try to hide it . . . he was a very important man. . . . I know for a fact that his dealings with the Middle East were at the highest level; he dealt with presidents and kings and was sought by everybody. . . . Members of the bar press were in the habit of checking inside stories with him. . . .

'He always drank a lot; they all do, God only knows why. He came to see me around 1981. It was rather unexpected because we weren't exactly friends and I found the fact that he telephoned me odd but I invited him for a drink at my place and he came right on time. He was thirsty and had two quick beers before he plunged into whisky . . .

'He spoke about the old days, how much fun he had at the bar . . . became teary-eyed and then cried. . . . Christ, I wasn't even a friend of his, as I said. . . . Then, out of the blue, he reached into his pocket and produced some gold tie clips and asked me whether I'd like to buy them. He was still crying.

'What the hell would I do with gold tie clips so I asked him why he needed to sell the tie clips . . . you'll never know what he said . . . to eat, that's what he said. . . . A man who a few years back was referred to as a kingmaker needed money to eat, wow! Well I gave him five hundred dollars and he gave me a post-dated cheque which bounced . . . Poor guy. . . .

'I began to ask around . . . he was in debt to everybody . . . he was reduced to a drunk, a small-time con man . . . his list of debts is long . . . old contacts tried to help; a former Lebanese president gave him money but you can't support someone like that all the time. . . .

'A good thing the Russians don't know about him – they'd go for him, try to recruit him. . . . I don't know . . . it's a sad situation . . . I don't understand the Americans; surely they could do something for him. After all he was very important. . . .'

I have checked on the former CIA agent in question and his recent life is nothing but a trail of bad cheques and phoney deals. My informer was right; the man had been a high-level CIA operative who never hid his identity and who had a weakness for the high life. He was fired in mysterious circumstances after a long, mostly successful, career and my informer's account is a good description of what has happened to him.

This man did not fall apart because he had been 'an under-cover agent'; he became undone because his CIA position afforded him status, the genuine exercise of power over people and governments. He, like many other CIA operatives, was given the world on a plate and had it taken away from him in a way that would break stouter spirits.

I cannot recollect a single case of this type regarding a British agent, no examples of Brits who, after being fired by MI6 or MI5 for incompetence, continued to pretend they were still employed by them – and Americans did. I know of no former MI6 operatives who became whores of the business, offering their services to those who could afford to pay, the way one former bar CIA operative went to work for Israel. Former MI6 agents have written books but, unlike the books of former bar CIA types, they stopped short of inflating their own importance and lying. The CIA does to some of its agents what Hollywood does to some of its stars: up, up, up and then down again with a crash. Could it be a manifestation of a deeper national malaise?

Whether you look at what the bar spies did to others or at what the game did to some of them, spying is a dirty and deadly game.

'Don't forget the business aspect of the bar. Businessmen who used it were as important as spies and journalists – perhaps more.'

Paul Parker, former Bank of America vice president

'What do you mean, were any business deals done there? All Middle East business was done there.'

Myrna Bustani, part owner, St George Hotel

'The oil people were there all the time, but so was everybody else.'

Lebanese journalist Hanna Ghossun

9

YES, MR GETTY

The tall, bespectacled young man noticed that the eyes of the concierge, betraying obvious surprise, shifted to the man standing next to him. As he turned to look, the man, without any preliminaries, asked, 'Are you Parker?'

'Yes, I am,' answered Bank of America vice president Paul Parker.

'Parker, I understand you're giving a cocktail party tonight. Would you like to invite me? Everyone in the Middle East I want to meet is going to be there.'

'Mr Getty, it would be an honour. Any time after six in the bar annexe, in the grill room. My wife and I look forward to seeing you.'

'Don't worry,' said Getty, walking away, 'I'll be there.'

It was the fall of 1957 and J. Paul Getty, who did not fly, had arrived in Beirut by ship to meet people important to the business of Getty Oil Co. That evening he arrived at the Parkers' party early, perfunctorily greeted Paul and his wife, Willa, and set about rearranging the chairs in the room in a way which focussed attention on where he sat. Just about everyone paid their respects to the legendary Mr Getty and some thought Parker had pulled a fast one by not telling them the party was in honour of the famous man.

The following day Getty summoned his Middle East general manager, Ed Brown, and ran through the list of people he had met at Parker's party. Mr Getty did not need to waste time travelling by ship to the various countries of the Middle East; he was right, everybody he wanted to meet was there. Ten years later, the same room was used for a party given by the Chase Manhattan Bank for their chairman, David Rockefeller.

The bar was indeed a place where the Gettys and Rockefellers went to meet everyone who mattered in the Middle East, including representatives of presumptuous new money. Among Parker's guests had been brokers, contractors, oil men, heads of various commercial offices and old Lebanese traders with a finger in every Middle East commercial pie. At the time of the Rockefeller party, in 1967, Beirut had more commercial banks than New York: it had become a recognized international business and financial centre with worldwide influence. The bar was the centre of the centre of this activity, the place favoured by the more important financiers and businessmen.

Beirut's – and the bar's – far-reaching influence became apparent as early as the mid-fifties. The Bank of America, Chase Manhattan Bank and Citibank (then First National of New York) were the first American banks to open Beirut branches, in 1955. Russ Smith, head of Bank of America International, came to Beirut that summer on a routine visit to their new branch. While staying at the hotel, Smith accidentally ran into his counterparts from Chase and Citibank, both in town for similar reasons.

The three bankers were friendly competitors and one evening they stopped at the bar for an after-dinner nightcap. Inevitably the subject of discussion turned to the huge amounts of dollar deposits their branches held from the governments and citizens of oil-rich countries, particularly Kuwait and Saudi Arabia. The interest rate the bankers had been paying their depositors was considerably lower than the rates in other financial centres. Smith wondered whether the Beirut deposits could finance a lowering of the prime rate in the United States. They all agreed that their banks could draw enough money out of Beirut to lower the prime rate by half a percentage point. The following day, their respective managements agreed with them and their banks had a reduction in interest rates which was followed by everyone.

Thereafter, bankers from all over the world watched the in and out flow of oil-country deposits and the shifts from one currency to another. I cannot recall a single week when a visiting banker did not appear at the bar to determine what was happening in these areas.

Four years later, in 1959, Volkswagen decided to enter the Middle East market. As a first step, the company sent one of its executive vice presidents to Beirut to locate competent distributors. Naturally, the man came to the bar, almost a precondition for studying the nuances of his assignment. There he met the answer to his prayers in Saudi business-man Ghazi Shaker, a polished, forward-looking man whose family already represented General Motors. Their three-day huddles in the bar were concluded by an agency agreement which changed the nature of the automobile business in the Middle East. The arrival of the inexpensive beetle created a new market which focussed on second cars and on young people, paving the way for the eventual arrival of Japanese imports.

Countless business deals were initiated, negotiated and concluded in the bar. Like visiting journalists, foreign businessmen used the place as a halfway house where they familiarized themselves with regional developments. And they turned it into an oasis where they met their Arab counterparts who, like them, preferred it to the staleness of Jeddah, Kuwait and Abu Dhabi. But, more than the ordinary business deals, however large, our concern, those which mirrored the bar's, is the interaction of international business, espionage and politics.

The 1965 collapse of Intra Bank provides a profound example. Intra, until then Lebanon's biggest commercial bank, was Palestinian-owned and run by the flamboyant, irreverant visionary, Yusuf Bedas. Intra controlled Middle East Airlines and the Casino du Liban, two huge sources of pride for the Lebanese, who saw in Palestinian control of their national assets an infringment of their economic sovereignty. Eventually, the Lebanese conspired against Intra and its management and unjustifiably denied it the funds to maintain liquidity, thus engineering its downfall.

The Russians, who, like everyone else, had an active

business presence in Beirut through Narodny Bank, saw in Intra's collapse an opportunity to penetrate the economy of the Middle East by acquiring the temporarily defunct bank or its major subsidiary, Middle East Airlines. Russian emissaries wasted no time in approaching Intra's major shareholder, Najib Salha, and Middle East Airlines' chairman, Najib Allumedine, with almost open-ended offers.

Simultaneously, Daniel Ludwig, an American millionaire, set up an improvised headquarters in the bar to do the same, to negotiate a deal for Intra or its airline or casino subsidiaries. Ludwig, normally a recluse, was so anxious to establish a foothold in Beirut that he operated in the open, speaking with the two principals contacted by the Russians and anyone else who might help. He went so far as to despatch Lebanese banker Carlos Arida to New York with an offer to Bedas of two million dollars in cash in return for his support. Refusing to accept that the bank would be liquidated, Bedas viewed the offer as a bribe and rejected it out of hand.

Analysing Ludwig's chances, Paul Parker decided that the Russians were determined to outbid him. Parker rushed to the US Embassy and informed the ambassador of the Russians' plans, painstakingly pointing out the likely repercussions of their success. The US Embassy in Beirut panicked. An embassy man came to the bar and told Ludwig to match any Russian offer as a holding action, while others contacted Intra's major shareholders to say that a US rescue effort more generous and beneficial than any Russian offer was on the way. The US government supported its embassy and delivered on its promise in record time. US investment bankers Kidder Peabody were hired to forestall any Russian takeover; they liquidated the bank after divesting it of its subsidiaries, which were successfully floated as independent companies. Intra would have been viable were it not for political machinations.

And so a major economic engagement between Russia and the US was secretly fought and won at the bar. A Russian victory would have affected the economic stability of Lebanon and the Middle East.

Though banking is occasionally of interest as an extension of politics, the arms trade is a business activity which always attracts the attention of spies and journalists. In the Middle East, armaments is a huge business which consumes on average one-third of national budgets. A big arms deal tells a great deal about both the purchaser and the supplier. Even today, an arms deal between Saudi Arabia and Russia would signal a major shift in policy with wide repercussions. Arms deals were negotiated, concluded and, occasionally, undone at the bar.

In 1974, Iraq decided to buy Western arms for the first time since the overthrow of its pro-Western monarchy in 1958, a major political development which revealed disaffection with its traditional arms supplier and political supporter, Russia. One of the items at the top of the Iraqis' hardware shopping list was helicopters, specifically the Lynx helicopter, a joint development by Westland Helicopters of the UK and Aerospatiale of France. Under their joint manufacturing agreement, Westland had responsibility for international sales. Another joint development of these two companies, the Gazelle helicopter, was marketed internationally by Aerospatiale. The two companies competed openly. When Iraqi feelers were put out to Westland for buying the Lynx, the French found out and proceeded to promote the Gazelle.

For this deal, the initial contact with Westland was undertaken on behalf of a Beirut-based Palestinian group. The Iraqis avoided direct contact because they feared that the UK would refuse to supply them with Lynx. Dealing through intermediaries would limit the potential damage to relations caused by such refusal; it would eliminate the need for an Iraqi reaction to it. On the other hand, the Beirut group was happy to act as middlemen and managed to obtain a commission agreement of ten per cent from Westland on all sales to Iraq; in this case, four million pounds sterling. To the amazement of all and joy of the intermediary group, the British government, seeing an opportunity to erode Russia's influence in Iraq, approved the sale.

Early in 1975, the London representative of the Beirut front group, who flew to Beirut to apprise his colleagues of the latest developments, stayed at the St George Hotel. He was to be followed there by John Speechily, a Westland director entrusted with finalizing the deal.

Sensing defeat, the French company dispatched a representative to Baghdad to change the mind of the Iraqi Ministry of Defence in favour of the Gazelle and sent another to Beirut to offer an enticing fifteen per cent commission.

Despite the tempting level of the French commission offer, the Beirut group wanted to close the Westland deal so as to avoid the pitfalls of uncertain delay. But they also feared that a blanket refusal to deal with the French would prompt the man in Baghdad to call on the French government for help. Among other things, the French government was capable of offering better credit terms. The representative of the Beirut group staying at the hotel met with the Aerospatiale man at the bar. He feigned interest in the French offer, but insisted that the man in Baghdad be withdrawn immediately because he was 'muddying the waters'.

A complex series of events took place as a result of what looked like non-stop meetings at the bar over a forty-eight-hour period. Aerospatiale withdrew its man from Baghdad. Simultaneously, Speechily was directed to Cairo, where two members of the Beirut group flew to meet him. The agreement was finalized in Cairo to be signed in Baghdad later, while the intermediary in the bar stalled Aerospatiale.

Upon receiving an all-clear telephone call from Cairo, the would-be buyer in the bar placed two calls to London. The first was to his stockbroker with instructions to buy Westland shares; the second to a friend who leaked the news of the Iraqis' deal to the London *Evening Standard*. When the *Evening Standard* ran the story in its financial section, the value of Westland shares went up by twenty per cent. By the time Aerospatiale's representative woke up to what was happening, it was too late for his company and government to do anything. It was a clean sweep for the Beirut group.

The 1965 British sale of military aircraft to Saudi Arabia stipulated a complex way of rewarding the inevitable intermediaries. While everybody took it for granted that money would change hands, King Faisal of Saudi Arabia and the British government were committed to the elimination of middlemen and their commissions.

This desire to avoid the bribe/commission was more than a wish to transact a clean deal; both sides knew that the Americans had been miffed because Britain was encroaching on a traditionally American market and would, to undermine future British deals, go out of their way to expose any 'corrupt' aspect of the British-Saudi cooperation. The bar press, aware that the initial part of the deal was worth over three hundred million dollars, tried in vain to determine the level of commission and the recipients.

A year and a half later, several members of the bar press were asked by their news organizations to verify reports originating in Rotterdam about Saudi sales of crude oil on the open market. Saudi Arabia denied the reports and oil experts in Beirut doubted their validity, but the reports persisted. At that time, unlike now, the sale of oil on the open market was a unique and major development, one which struck at the heart of oil agreements between governments and the major oil companies. All manner of interpretation greeted this news, including the claim that Saudi Arabia, the world's number one oil exporter, was about to nationalize its oil industry to punish the oil companies of America for the latter's support of Israel.

The truth lay somewhere between Saudi Arabian denials and the persistence of the rumours. Saudi Arabia had not changed its oil policy and was not out to undermine the oil companies and punish America. A Lebanese member of the bar press solved the mystery but, because of long-standing friendly relations with Saudi Arabia, did not write the story.

The Saudis had agreed to barter oil for aeroplanes. The Saudi Ministry of Defence crowd, which had been denied its commission by the stubbornness of King Faisal and the British, got around the problem by understating the value of their oil, saying that it would take more oil to buy each plane than it actually did. They diverted the rest to Rotterdam and sold it there to realize their commission of tens of millions of dollars.

Unable to get to the bottom of the story, the bar press, all except our silent friend, explained the stoppage of Rotterdam oil sales by saying that Saudi Arabia had decided to avoid a final break with the US, that someone in the US had talked Saudi Arabia out of the foolishness of 'destroying' the oil companies. In fact, the Saudis stopped selling oil on the open market after the barter part of the deal was finished.

Disunity has become a trademark of modern Arab politics, and also characterizes Arab governments' treatment of common commercial interests, even when cooperation and agreement might produce results beneficial to the participants. Sheikh Najib Allumedine, for over twenty years chairman of the Board of Middle East Airlines and a frequent visitor to the bar, is as good an authority on this subject as any man alive. His experiences in the field are legendary and much of what happened in this typical story of Arab failure took place at the St George bar and its environs.

By the early sixties, the Lebanese-owned Middle East Airlines was recognized as one of the best-run airlines in the world, while the other Arab countries were either expanding or creating their national flag carriers. To the forward-looking Allumedine, it was time for inter-Arab cooperation. A few years earlier, the talented Lebanese had used the weight of his reputation as the grand old man of the regional airline business to create the Arab Air Carriers Organization (AACO). He sought to organize pan-Arab maintenance facilities, a central spare parts warehousing operation and, eventually, a unified policy toward pricing and dealing with non-Arab airlines. Allumedine wanted to create the 'strongest possible airline group in the world'.

Sheikh Najib saved his ambitious plan until AACO had one of its regularly scheduled meetings in Beirut, where he would be host and the atmosphere would give the plan a totally Lebanese flavour. The meeting, like most high-powered meetings in the Lebanese capital, took place at the St George.

The presentation of his plan was remarkable, covering everything from direct financial benefits to Arab dreams of exercising absolute power over their enterprise and considerable influence over the rights of foreign airlines to operate in their territory. The delegates were awestruck; they were face to face with something more substantial than the empty rhetoric of their politicians. Discussion of the daring proposal took place over lunch in the grill room, every delegate vying with the next to express their support for the plan. No one took exception to the plan or any of its provisions, and the following day the press in Beirut and other Arab capitals accorded it front-page treatment. Then the Western press rightly described it as an ambitious plan with far-reaching economic implications for the Arabs and those who trade with them.

For many years thereafter Sheikh Najib tried. One would see the lonely figure of the urbane man, huddled in a corner of the bar with the representative of an Arab airline, still trying to breathe life into a non-political business deal which would help every Arab country. Unfortunately, because each director had a vested interest in the purchases of his airline, nothing ever came of Sheikh Najib's plan. Says he with obvious pain, 'They all said yes but no one would do anything. . . . I finally got tired of it all.' What happened to Allumedine's plan in the bar, microcosm of the Middle East, is a good example of Arab non-cooperation, an inability to follow words with deeds and an inertia which appears inherent in their national character.

10

A BRIBE AS BIG
AS THE ST GEORGE

International business and international politics are so closely intertwined that it can be difficult to separate the two, and no more so than in the Middle East, where the West's global strategy relies on a continuing supply of the region's only main export. The vulnerability of this strategy was exposed by the oil embargo of the early seventies to everyone who had to queue for petrol.

Joe Ellender, top government relations officer of the oil company Aramco, was jokingly known to bar regulars as Haji Yusuf, pilgrim Joseph. Ellender spoke impeccable Arabic and carried himself with the serenity of a true believer who had made the pilgrimage to Mecca. He liked his nickname as much as others enjoyed using it. Ellender the pilgrim was a shrewd intelligence officer whose nominal job with Aramco was to liaise with various Saudi Arabian government departments and, by keeping them and the Saudi central government happy, help maintain the highly successful business enterprise of American oil interests and simultaneously guard the West's strategic interests.

Ellender's job demanded that he shuttle between Aramco's corporate headquarters in New York and its field centre in Dahran, Saudi Arabia. He invariably stopped at the bar, where his Southern gentleman's manners and Yale education endeared him to one and all; he was folksy and friendly, but sharp enough to engage the astute journalists in discussion about the destructiveness of sudden oil wealth on the social structure in the Arab world. People liked Haji Yusuf, but until now little has been revealed about his important espionage activities. Abu Saïd is the source for the following details

118

about a major Ellender operation to protect America's oil interests.

Haji Yusuf's stops at the bar during the summer of 1966 were more frequent than usual and he courted Abu Saïd with obvious deliberateness. Abu Saïd knew something was afoot for, though the two had known each other for some time, Haji Yusuf obviously had something specific in mind.

Ellender's preoccupation was eventually revealed: he wanted Abu Saïd to act as an intermediary between himself and Abdallah Tariki, the former Saudi Minister of Petroleum and Mineral Resources. Saudi Arabia's King Faisal had fired Tariki, accusing his oil minister of attempts to undermine his country's special relationship with the US. Tariki, insisting that his only goal was better oil deals for Saudi Arabia, had moved to Beirut to avoid arrest and imprisonment. From his exile in Beirut, Tariki had assumed the rôle of leading critic of Saudi Arabian and Aramco oil policies, publishing a stream of newspaper and magazine articles in local publications and making himself available to the bar press.

At first Haji Yusuf, who often saw Tariki at the bar but limited himself to a distant wave, as befit the representative of an enemy group, asked Abu Saïd about Tariki's aims. Tariki's campaign hinged on his allegations that Aramco was not using proper conservation methods to protect Saudi oil fields and that Aramco was lying about its production figures. He viewed the Saudi royal family as co-conspirators concerned only for their own pockets and not the rights of the Saudi people. Tariki's former employees at the ministry had secretly kept him informed of up-to-date developments. Along with most enlightened Saudis, they adored Tariki and supported him against Aramco and their own profligate rulers. There was nothing new in what Abu Saïd told Haji Yusuf.

But Ellender was already aware of Tariki's work; his half-hearted attempts to stop publication of Tariki's articles had failed. Tariki had become a thorn in the side of the Aramco-Saudi alliance and his well-documented accusations were repeated everywhere. The bar press labelled him an 'oil nationalist'.

Haji Yusuf had no option; he had to try to silence Tariki. When he solicited Abu Saïd's help and asked, in a flat, matter-of-fact way, whether Abu Saïd would act as a go-between, Abu Saïd, anxious to discontinue the dialogue, gave a tentative yes. He wanted to know what was required of him. 'Well,' said Ellender without any sense of drama, 'we are willing to pay him five million dollars in cash to keep quiet, to stop writing and speaking.'

A dumbfounded Abu Saïd shook his head in despair, for not only did he know that Tariki was not bribable, that he put principle above money, but he was disappointed in Ellender's crude approach. He refused to play intermediary, stating that the nature of the request endangered his relationship with the Saudi exile. But Ellender, obviously operating under considerable pressure, literally refused to take no for an answer and countered with, 'What about fifteen million dollars, that's enough money to buy this hotel – we want him off our backs; he is doing a lot of damage.' Abu Saïd was aghast but adamant and even the prospect of his own fee of two hundred and fifty thousand dollars didn't appeal to him. A disappointed Haji Abdallah left the bar and Beirut for Saudi Arabia mumbling something about there being more than one way to skin a cat.

Two days after his dramatic meeting with Haji Yusuf, Abu Saïd was drinking with Tariki. In the middle of one of their ordinary conversations he used the ploy of a hypothetical question to ask Tariki what his reaction would be if oil interests offered him tens of millions of dollars to stop his campaign against them. A pained Tariki characteristically turned the question around: 'Abu Saïd, would you want me to accept a bribe?' Both men agreed that the offer, if it existed, should be turned down.

Soon after, Tariki's bar and Beirut activities came to a sudden end. The Lebanese government, shamefully discarding its traditional role as a haven for all shades of Middle East political opinion, deported him, claiming that his continued presence 'endangered brotherly relations with Saudi Arabia'. A heartbroken Tariki moved to Algeria, whence he continued

Above: The St George Hotel in 1971.
Below: Aerial view of the hotel (right foreground, on the waterfront), 1974. The semicircular area to the left of the building is the bar terrace.

Right: Head barman Ali Bitar.
Below: Jean Bertolet, the hotel's general manager from 1961 to 1969 (right), greeting King Muhammad Zahir Shah of Afghanistan (left) and Lebanese Premier Rashid Karameh (centre), August 1963. Middle Eastern leaders visiting Beirut usually stayed at the hotel.

Above: A press conference in the hotel bar. In the corner is Abu Saïd, with Claire Hollingworth of the *Daily Telegraph* on his left, next to her Sam Pope Brewer of the *New York Times* and on the far right Peter Duffield of the *Daily Express.*
Below: Lebanese presidential hopeful Raymond Edde and US diplomat and agent Mary Hawthorne. They often met at the bar.

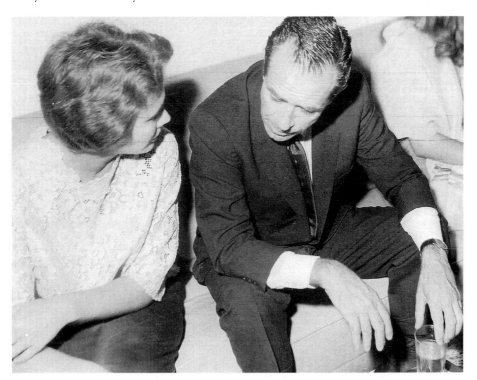

Above: The author (centre) introducing the press corps to King Hussein of Jordan at Basman Palace in Amman, 1959.
Left: Intra Bank chairman Yusuf Bedas. Part of the plot to destroy the bank was hatched in the hotel bar.

The author with Nicole Cuvellier of 'Green with Money' fame, in front of the Beirut court house where her trial was being held.

Left: Sheikh Najib Allumedine, chairman of Middle East Airlines. *Below:* Sheikh Najib Allumedine at a meeting of the Arab Air Carriers Organization.

Left: Myrna Bustani, part owner of the hotel.
Below: Myrna Bustani taking her seat in the Lebanese parliament.

Above: The St George Hotel under fire in 1976.
Below: After an attack, smoke billows from the hotel windows. The car windscreens have been shattered by the blast.

his activities without fear that its government, too, would succumb to Saudi pressure.

Rumours circulating around the bar intimated that a bribe of millions of dollars lay behind the deportation. Even the president of Lebanon was implicated, though no concrete evidence of this has ever been provided – just the knowledge that it would have taken a great deal to compromise the country's traditional neutrality. Abu Saïd listened to the rumours with a bitter smile. He always wondered whether the Lebanese got their perfidy's worth or whether they settled for a mere five million. Ellender has since been exposed as a CIA agent. Whether the offer involved intelligence money or oil money is not known; perhaps this was a coordinated effort.

The world next heard about Tariki during the 1973 oil crisis, the one provoked by a threefold increase in oil prices. He had become a consultant to Colonel Gadafi of Libya and, having correctly assessed the supply-demand dynamics, he is reported to have told Gadafi: 'Hit them [the oil companies], hit them now and hit them hard.' He got his own back.

Garry Owen was head of the Aramco department that Ellender had worked for, an important, sensitive position. Owen, like Ellender, was a bar regular, and was known for soliciting journalists' opinions about Middle Eastern events while briefing them on the good state of relations between Aramco and its host government. Though we know of no direct connection between Owen and the CIA, reciprocity between Aramco and the CIA is common knowledge – the importance of Aramco and oil to America dictated cooperation.

The Middle East was, and remains, a place where American and British oil interests competed and clashed, both openly and secretly. The British were there first, winning oil concessions because of their dominant political position and special relationships with rulers in places like Iran, Iraq and Kuwait. The Americans, whose big prize was Saudi Arabia, came later, and they prided themselves on managing their oil interests in accordance with commercial considerations unconnected to politics. By the time this ceased to be the case, they had replaced the Brits as the area's leading oil concessionaire. Each side was in the business of exposing the other's unwholesome practices in an attempt to win favour with the area's governments and peoples, and each guarded its oil agreements religiously. But the Americans always claimed that they paid a higher price for oil than did the Brits, who pointedly reminded the Arabs of America's support for 'Israeli expansionism'.

In the early fifties, Iran, recovering from a period of political turmoil, sought to renegotiate its oil arrangements with the British. The Americans wanted the oil concession for themselves and counted on inherent Iranian anti-British feelings. The considerable behind-the-scenes jockeying between the rival governments came into the open in 'the field'.

Sometime during 1954 Garry Owen and three colleagues, on their way to the US from Saudi Arabia, entered the bar equipped with the usual heavy, document-laden briefcases, exchanged greetings with some bar journalists, had a few drinks and retired to the grill room for lunch. Two hours later, dapper grill room manager Cezar Granselle went looking for them with a thick brown envelope in his hand, but they were nowhere to be found. At a loss, Granselle went into the bar and entrusted it to a correspondent friend of Owen's.

Back home with the envelope, the American correspondent fell victim to curiosity, if only because the envelope had so many seals. When he opened it and examined its contents, he was flabbergasted: he was in possession of copies of the most recent oil agreement between Aramco and Saudi Arabia, on the face of it original documents with the king's signature. He knew enough to recognize a milestone agreement which stipulated a higher royalty to Saudi Arabia than had hitherto existed.

Having resisted the temptation to use the material for a news story, our friend rushed to the US Embassy the following day to see one of the intelligence boys. Despite his strenuous protestations, nobody was available and the journalist settled for giving the envelope to a senior secretary in return for a hand-written receipt.

Initially, the secretary was reluctant to become involved, and agreed only after opening the envelope herself and almost fainting on reading its contents. Demonstrating on-the-spot initiative she advised that five hundred Lebanese lira (then one hundred and fifty dollars) should be paid to Granselle as a reward for his honesty. She later made good her promise to reimburse him as soon as she got the envelope to its rightful owner.

Two months later Joe Goodwin, CIA station chief in Tehran, passed through Beirut and naturally stopped in at the bar. The American correspondent who had returned the envelope was known to Goodwin, who joined him for a drink. At the end of a lengthy conversation Goodwin questioned the man about the envelope, its contents and whether he had shared them with anyone. As he left, he jokingly scolded the correspondent for his honesty because 'it cost the United States dearly'.

What really happened was a strange series of mishaps in a bungled intelligence operation. The documents were forgeries, left behind by design. Normally, the documents would have found their way to Iran and either the Iranians would have insisted on equal terms which, if realized, would make British oil companies less profitable; or the Brits and the Iranians would have failed to reach agreement, thus opening the door for American oil entry into Iran. In either case, their exposure would muddy the waters between Britain and Iran.

Nobody counted on Granselle's honesty: they supposed anything left behind would be sold and eventually exposed. In addition, the choice of the American journalist was a disaster: he was a CIA agent who used the embassy in an act of desperation because he personally had no way of repatriating the documents speedily, though he eventually wrote his own secret report recommending punishment for the careless people. The embassy secretary, unlike the desk officer, who would have some inkling of what was afoot, acted with bravery because she saw in the situation a chance to do something big which would contribute to her career.

Just in case, there was a lot of back tracking. Poor Granselle was accused of stealing the documents from one of the briefcases of one of the Aramco men. He and everyone regretted his honesty. Everyone, that is, except the British oil man who showed up at the bar from nowhere for two weeks of rest and recreation. He was full of smiles.

Oil politics and oil company shenanigans are not the only field where politics and business merge. Another business area mired in politics is that of trade with Israel. The Arab Boycott Office, a branch of the Arab League, is entrusted with the Arab boycott of companies trading with Israel. One by-law of this organization permits dealings with such 'culprits' when their products or services or both are decreed to be of 'strategic importance'. In other words, a company blacklisted by the Arab League can overcome this hurdle if a host country determines that there is no equal or substitute for what it has to offer, and that its products are demonstrably superior to anything offered by others.

The Ford Motor Company had a small manufacturing plant in Israel, making it subject to the boycott and its exceptions. Representatives of the Ford Motor Company habitually visited Beirut and the bar to petition to have their name struck from the blacklist because the Israeli plant was small and unimportant, and to formulate products which could be considered of 'strategic' importance. Their frequent trips to Beirut were unsuccessful, until a Ford representative ran into Shehadeh Twal of Jordan.

A Jordanian Christian descendant of the leaders of the town of Maddabah, Twal was a successful businessman whose corruption was part of a belief in the corruption of the Middle East and its governments. Several bar visits with the Ford people convinced him that whatever strategic considerations might be needed to get Ford off the blacklist could be arranged – for the right price. Over endless drinks of Black Label, the Arab's favourite alcoholic drink, he signed an agency agreement to sell Ford products to the Jordanian government.

In Jordan, Twal and his friends proceeded to fabricate the strategic reasons and have them adopted by the government. It took six months for the Jordanian Ministry of Defence to issue an elaborate set of requirements for the procurement of trucks for the army which fortunately showed that Ford trucks were perfect for the terrain; no other product was suitable.

The bar became a regular meeting place between important Jordanians and Ford executives. The Ford people, converted to believers in the art of the possible, tried to promote their civilian products, but even Twal's corrupt entourage could not come up with satisfactory reasons. The only civilian cars to enter Jordan were used by the families of the inventors of the strategic reasons which facilitated the sale of army trucks. They were presents from super-agent Twal and were not even considered a bribe by US officials who, opposed as they are to the Arab Boycott Office, welcomed anything done to undermine it.

Ford was lucky – its agent did deliver the goods. Boeing, which had no blacklist problems, came to the bar seeking a regional representative, someone who would be effective throughout the diverse countries of the Middle East. Business and bar legend favoured a Lebanese national because of the country's political neutrality and the Lebanese people's superior trading talents.

What the Boeing representative failed to gauge was the extent to which people might recommend someone to serve their own purpose instead of Boeing's interests and how much political weight there could be behind such recommendations. When the Boeing man put out his feelers in the bar he was approached by two former Lebanese cabinet members who wanted to advise him.

Both honourable men carried a lot of influence in Lebanon, both spoke to him in reasonable terms and both recommended one S.B., a bar regular who spoke three languages fluently, was an impeccable dresser and appeared to know the ins and outs of Middle Eastern business through his representation of lesser companies in the area. The number of people recommending and vouching for Badr increased, all but overwhelming the Boeing man. On the strength of this and interviews with the man himself, Badr was appointed agent for the whole of the Middle East.

The problems between S.B. and Boeing began immediately when the agent told Boeing he could not spare the time to travel to other Arab countries. His political commitments as a Lebanese member of parliament precluded lengthy absences, but he still expected a commission on Boeing's universally needed products. Both the orders for planes and the ensuing commissions were substantial.

It took a mere four months for Boeing to discover what had happened and for professionalism to surface. The men who had recommended S.B. were fellow members of parliament who had been promised his vote on several critical parliamentary issues in return for their recommendation. Boeing's business had been subordinated to a barter deal in local politics.

Badr was paid a substantial amount of money to cede the agency agreement after his commissions had exceeded the salary of Boeing's chairman. When the Boeing representative complained about the results to one of the local politicians who had recommended Badr, he replied, 'He just doesn't like to fly.'

These are but a few examples of how business and politics mated to produce big, intricate bar business/political stories. Now that the bar is no more, the same game still takes place all over the Middle East, but the participants don't have the panache of the original players.

11
ROGUES

Unlike journalism or espionage, with their behind-the-scenes and mysterious activities, business affairs are supposed to be open, better-reported and easier for the average person to understand. This is not true. Some games played in the business world of the bar compare with the darkest, biggest and ugliest of reporting and spying.

Intra Bank, because of its Palestinian ownership and management, was the constant target of rumours spread by many Lebanese and others who resented its success and equated its fortunes with those of the PLO. The same people who opposed the PLO and the Palestinians opposed Intra, and many of the rumours against the bank started in the bar.

One such rumour was started by a well-known Lebanese banker, a competitor of Intra. Already known to many of the bar regulars, the man inexplicably became a frequent visitor in 1965. During this time he made a special effort to whisper in the ear of a young correspondent that Intra was facing a liquidity crisis. The emir of Kuwait, one of the biggest depositors in Intra, was summering in Lebanon at the time and so the informer suggested that the young correspondent check with the emir about 'the safety of his money'.

Realizing there was potential for a big story, the young correspondent managed to disturb the emir's annual rest. He echoed his informer's question without attribution but the Kuwaiti ruler, a major Intra depositor, was in the dark regarding Intra's financial condition and he received an unprintable answer, though the emir's disquiet was clear.

The emir was sufficiently concerned to summon Intra chairman Yusuf Bedas in order to withdraw five million dollars in cash, his spur-of-the-moment way of checking on the financial soundness of Intra. The request was stupid but Bedas, always inventive, put the money in suitcases and delivered it to the emir's summer residence within thirty-six hours. The Arab chieftain, embarrassed, refused Bedas's offer to have his assistants count the money and apologetically asked Bedas to take it back. Bedas refused; he stomped out of the sheikh's summer palace muttering the equivalent of 'you can take your money and – '

The intemperate Bedas won the day in terms of proving the soundness of the bank's finances, but lost an important customer. Then other Kuwaitis pulled their money out in sympathy with their head of state. It did not stop there; Intra's enemy temporarily changed tactics and became fond of pointing out Bedas's haughtiness to depositors from the oil-rich countries, the type of people who cherished personal attention, something Bedas supposedly lacked.

Within two years there was a run on the deposits of Intra Bank and bands of Lebanese bankers descended on the bar to propagandize against Intra. Neither the bar press nor the public could ignore the accusations. The bank's assets far exceeded its liabilities, but the Lebanese Central Bank, very much part of a conspiracy to rid the country of Palestinian commercial influence, refused to advance it funds. Intra Bank collapsed.

The collapse of Intra Bank undermined confidence in the Lebanese banking system. After all, the Central Bank should have guarded against the liquidity crisis, if indeed there was one. Its failure to come to Intra's aid made rich Gulf Arabs shy of depositing money in Lebanese banks, naturally considered unsafe when the leading commercial bank of the country failed.

Some of the Lebanese bankers, businessmen and journalists who engineered Intra's downfall met at the bar to celebrate the event with champagne; bar press members who innocently helped bring about Intra's end participated in the festivities. Years later it was confirmed that Intra's assets had been sound and well in excess of its liabilities.

One bar journalist, having determined that one conspirator was prompted to action by Bedas's refusal to appoint him to Intra's board and another had owed Intra money which he couldn't repay, mused: 'Let's face it – we were used. It was a conspiracy beyond our comprehension – billions of dollars were lost.'

Smaller, apolitical business frauds also found a home at the bar. There was a little Armenian who frequented the bar almost every day, usually between one and two in the afternoon. He was slightly over five feet tall, dressed in Our-Man-in-Havana tropical suits, sported a monocle and had a permanent boyish smile on his face. He always drank two or three whiskys quickly, in about fifteen minutes, and told a joke or two at the expense of his absent wife while he massaged his hand through his hair: 'My eyesight is getting bad, I just saw someone fatter than my wife.'

This ritual went on for years; the man became a fixture – a bar character – though little about him was known except that he was a wealthy antiquarian. On rare occasions people would ask him about something they had bought or were about to buy and he would answer lightly, successfully dispensing with taking his opinion and trade seriously.

In 1965 the wily little Armenian, using the same endearing smile, approached a foreign correspondent to tell him of a rare antique find, a Phoenician vase, which he was trying to sell. Discretion was essential; the vase was so rare the Lebanese government was unlikely to let it out of the country. Having paid a considerable amount of money for it, he wanted to sell it at a modest profit – before the Lebanese government found out.

The foreign correspondent, who fancied himself a collector, arranged to see the vase and was stunned by its beauty. He agreed to help.

The Metropolitan Museum of New York was tipped off by the foreign correspondent's employer, who had been told the size, shape and period of the find. The Met people were indeed interested and the man they sent to the bar was a most unlikely visitor, a US Eastern establishment scholar with the sedate air of academe. The correspondent, excited by the prospect of involvement in something big relating to his hobby, vouched for the Armenian beyond his knowledge of the man. The Armenian's charm worked. The Met representative departed after ensuring that a specialist to authenticate the vase was on the way – another unusual visitor to the bar.

It took all of three weeks and the deal was done; the price was two million dollars. The Armenian had managed to convince the Met that he had refused a slightly higher offer in order to guarantee the proper home for this rarest of finds. He arranged to have the vase carried from Beirut to New York by a special messenger.

Three years later, the vase was uncovered as a fake. A bar player had, with the help of a bar journalist, cheated the Met out of two million dollars. Whether the correspondent was financially involved is not known. What we do know is that the stuffy experts of the Met were no match for the bar players. Even in this esoteric corner of the business world the bar produced the big deal. The Armenian claimed that he had merely fronted for the true owner of the vase and the truth of the whole episode was lost in a maze of claim and counter-claim. Jokes barman Ali Bitar: 'Maybe it was his eyesight – he always claimed it was poor.'

In the Middle East, politics and espionage themselves are often reduced to a service business. An elementary way to make money around the bar was to convince an intelligence service of one's capability to undertake a desired activity on their behalf, whether propagandizing, buying politicians, selling specific pieces of information or undermining enemies in a serious way. President Nasser, King Hussein of Jordan, King Faisal of Saudi Arabia, Syrian President Adib Shaishakly and Iraqi Premier Nuri Saïd, among others, at one point or another bought the loyalties of bar regulars to operate in these sordid fields.

A fascinating example of this enterprise is the story of Safa Eddine Orfally, an Iraqi. Safa came from an old, established family, had a law degree and at one point owned Baghdad's first supermarket. His practice of law was an on-and-off affair and he made noises purporting to show an interest in politics which no one took seriously because he had a more manifest interest in Black Label and pretty girls. Safa's saving grace was an abundance of charm.

In the early sixties, Safa lived in Beirut and immediately became a bar regular. It was his kind of place and he went there to meet fellow Iraqis as well as journalists and the others he quickly befriended. Initially Safa's presence in Beirut was meant to be temporary, an escape from the daily pressures of the socialist régime in his country. But the engaging atmosphere of Beirut, teeming with Iraqi political exiles opposed to the same régime, attracted him. He soon decided to stay in Beirut and become a political exile.

The Iraqi exiles with whom Safa met regularly at the bar were a pro-Nasser group who wished to replace their government with a régime that would follow their idol. One time, when members of this group, all Black Label whisky drinkers, decided to go to Cairo to meet Nasser to discuss their future moves on his behalf, Safa prevailed on them to take him along. After all, the Orfally name was well known and in the Middle East your family name or tribal connection is what matters.

As usual, the exiles exaggerated their chances of serving Nasser, made promises they couldn't possibly meet and asked for more money to continue their activities, 'the struggle against tyranny'. Safa put on a dazzling performance which so impressed Nasser that he gave Safa twice the amount of money he gave to the others – Safa promised at least twice as much as any of them did.

The Safa who returned to the St George Hotel Bar was even more generous than before – he was flush with funds. His compatriots shook their heads in utter despair as Safa regaled the bar press corps and anybody who cared to listen with stories about Egypt, the strength of the Egyptian armed forces and coming changes in the Middle East, exaggerating and inventing every step of the way. He saw himself as a Nasser protégé, and certainly his bar spokesman, but eventually the bar press and Nasser decided Safa was a most engaging rascal. Nasser would not give him any more money, while the seasoned bar press continued to enjoy his company without taking him seriously. Initially, they had been misled into writing several stories based on information from Safa which proved hugely inflated, if not totally wrong.

Safa's response to Nasser's action in cutting him off was telling: 'How does he expect to start a revolution without spending? Revolutions cost money.' And with that he sat at the bar and began telling the bar press about all Nasser's mistakes and the insensitivity of his régime to the wishes of fellow Arabs. His brief foray into the area of Middle East politics ended when he returned to Baghdad and his supermarket. Poor Nasser.

Nasser was not the only Arab political leader to fall for rogues who successfully exchanged political loyalty for money. King Hussein of Jordan suffered a worse fate because the schemer who cheated him out of money succeeded in his ploy for a long time and took Hussein for much more than Orfally got from Nasser.

R.A. was a second-string Lebanese journalist who envied the good fortune of his more successful colleagues and who was determined to emulate it, regardless of method or means. He became a bar regular and let it be known to visiting Arab dignitaries that he was a journalist for hire, available to advance the cause of any Arab country which would pay him for his efforts.

The Saudis, Iraqis and others initially approached by R.A. turned him down because they had 'better' Lebanese journalists available to them. Eventually, after months of trying, our friend met at the bar with the Jordanian Minister of Information, to whom he repeated his well-rehearsed offer. As King Hussein's policies were under attack by most Middle Eastern newspapers, Jordanian needs were greater than most. Lengthy bar negotiations resulted in an agreement that enabled our friend to start his own newspaper – which made no secret of its support of King Hussein's point of view.

Jordan, never a wealthy country, was using 'special funds'

to support R.A. There was only one problem; because of poor editorial quality and the lack of affection for its politics, no one bought the newspaper or advertised in it. A dangerous situation was developing; Hussein had to be convinced he was getting his money's worth.

R.A. responded to this danger in several ways. First, he convinced Hussein and Jordanian officialdom to grant him exclusive interviews on a regular basis; then he carried free advertising and finally he organized phoney purchases of his newspaper. The exclusives worked for a while, then people got tired of Jordanian officials repeating themselves; the discovery of the free advertising damaged whatever reputation the paper had established, but the phoney sales continued. What R.A. did was have newspaper boys give free copies to doormen, taxi drivers and the like. Meanwhile, he was in the bar on a regular basis, blowing his own trumpet about increased circulation and the influence of his publication with the masses.

The truth about R.A.'s newspaper was known to the bar press, who had never liked him and who viewed his presence among them as a poor reflection on their reputation, an attitude which brought about his eventual undoing.

A down-to-earth American journalist was having a chat in the bar with R.A.'s chief mentor, the Jordanian minister of information. Wishing that the Jordanian would do more to promote their pro-Western image, the journalist advised His Excellency to get a local paper to advance the Jordan point of view. But, observed His Excellency, we have a good newspaper and editor, R.A. and his publication. The newsman told the minister what he knew of R.A. and was stunned to hear the minister say that they had received reports to that effect, but had not believed them. Because the American was trying to be helpful and had no axe to grind, he was believed.

Jordan cut off R.A. and his newspaper folded shortly afterwards. It had cost King Hussein's government hundreds of thousands of dollars, most of which went to line the pockets of R.A., who, like Orfally, tried to change and find a new sponsor – luckily, without success.

The ultimate foolproof money-making scheme perpetrated by a bar character lasted nearly twelve years and might have continued to this day had the life of the bar itself not come to an end. A.-R.B. was another Iraqi with impressive lineage, a descendant of one of the country's oldest families which, along with Saudi Arabia's House of Saud, traced its ancestry to the Eniza tribe. A short, somewhat overweight man with a moustache, endearing bedouin manners and a little boy's giggle, this man, who spoke no foreign language, managed to parley his acquaintance with the foreign bar press into millions of dollars without ever a hint of what he was doing.

What A.-R.B. possessed was native bedouin guile and entry to the royal households of the Arabian peninsula. Naturally, he referred to members of the Saudi royal family as cousins, but he knew the ruling Sabah family in Kuwait, the sheikhs of Abu Dhabi, Dubai and Qatar and the sultan of Oman. They received him as the son of an old, honoured family and he carried himself accordingly.

When the monstrous scheme occured to A.-R.B. is unknown, but Ali Bitar, Khaldoun Solh, my father and I remember him well. Using his few words of English in the endearing way people do who speak languages badly, he would sit in the bar, buying drinks and making a point of meeting foreign journalists. To the bar press, he was a nice little man who seemed to know everyone in the Arabian Peninsula and who volunteered to get correspondents visas and interviews, the two items uppermost in their minds. All he asked was for two or three calling cards from each journalist. He had persistence; he never allowed a single foreign correspondent to pass through the bar without saying hello to them, always enquiring about their health, their families and their immediate needs. He was a check-grabber – always wanting to pay for every drink – but after all, he was supposed to be a sheikh.

But A.-R.B.'s most important activity was to obtain visas and interviews for people who asked for them. He always made it seem that he was doing both interviewer and interviewee a favour. Then, pushing his modicum of English into uncharted territory, he would follow up with the journalist, asking 'You say good things about the king/emir/sheikh?' When the answer was in the affirmative, he would buy a copy of the publication in question, have it translated, then journey with original and translation to see the chieftain in question and make a present of the article, all the time exaggerating the importance of the publication in which it had appeared.

What followed is in line with the corrupt practices of these courts: A.-R.B. would be compensated for his efforts in arranging publication of a favourable article. According to my investigation, the payments ranged between thirty thousand and one hundred thousand dollars per article. Often, after he managed to arrange two or three articles in praise of the same leader, he would ask for and be placed on a hefty retainer, all without the knowledge or suspicion of his journalist friends.

One of the more intriguing aspects of this man's manipulative nature was his ability to take the credit for favourable articles and to dissociate himself from unfavourable ones. There is no doubt in my mind that he understood English much better than he spoke it and had the uncanny ability to couch his presentations of his work in a most acceptable manner; he had all the heads of state of the Arabian Peninsula playing his game. I last saw A.-R.B. in Qatar; I ran into him accidentally while he was waiting to see the emir of the country. He greeted me effusively and said: 'I miss the St George Bar and all my journalist friends.' I bet he does.

Another who used his good family name for personal gain was Tawfiq Toukan, a member of one of the oldest, best-known and most influential and respected families in Palestine. Though he used his name to make money around the bar in the same way Safa Eddine Orfally and A.-R.B. did, his scheme was short-lived and its end very tragic.

The Toukans are in politics; many of them have been members of Jordanian cabinets and they have a solid constituency around the city of Nablus, which follows them blindly wherever they steer it. Their importance is so widely recognized that King Hussein's marriage to a Toukan bolstered his popularity. (His popular, attractive queen died tragically in a helicopter crash.) Any Arab politician hoping to woo the Palestinian world takes the Toukans into account.

Tawfiq was the black sheep of the family, a source of embarrassment to those who carried the proud name. He wandered around Europe, extracting fees from companies seeking a name to promote their fortunes in the Arab world, then, after exhausting that source, he came to Beirut in the early sixties to try his luck. For his like, the St George and its bar were the natural place to be.

By then an experienced con man, Tawfiq's first act was to leave fifty thousand dollars in bills with the cashier because he 'didn't want to wander around with that type of money in his pocket'. The story got out and became known throughout the hotel and the bar. He telephoned himself from various parts of Beirut pretending to be a prince, sheikh or businessman. He would leave messages for himself in the names of important people and collect them upon his return to the hotel. Within two weeks the image he sought to create was established: a Toukan with lots of money and connections with important people.

Tawfiq would send cablegrams to Arab heads of state. Using any event involving the Palestinians as pretext, he would cable President Nasser of Egypt or King Saud of Saudi Arabia with his views, offering congratulations for something they had done, asking them to note some observation or even requesting a meeting. With the Toukan name on the cablegram, the Arab leaders often responded, sometimes employing the Arab courtesy of addressing him as Brother. T.T., as he was known, would then walk into the bar with these cablegrams in hand and pass them around for everyone to see, the final confirmation that he was an important person and a big-time player.

Having created the proper background atmosphere, Toukan went for the kill. Yes, he could get someone in to see King Saud to discuss an oil concession. Of course Iraq needed to build a new pipeline and he could help a construction company to get a piece of the project. There was nothing to arranging favourable terms for buying phosphate from Jordan. There was nothing Toukan could not do and, because businessmen of all types stopped at the bar in pursuit of the crock of gold at the end of the rainbow, he managed to sign a number of agreements which guaranteed him hefty retainers from some of the more reputable companies in the world.

As luck would have it, an English businessman who had known Toukan in London appeared at the bar and felt compelled to share his previous unhappy experiences of the con man with a number of people. The story spread like wildfire, but this was of little help to companies which had already paid Toukan. After all, their contracts with him simply stated that he would 'use his influence' without stipulating what that influence might be and without requiring any guarantee of delivery of things promised.

Toukan left Beirut for Europe a richer man, but far from a repentant one. Later, in Paris, his trickery got completely out of control and he conned the Israeli government into accepting him as head of a pro-Israeli Palestinian government. With both the PLO and Mossad determined to eliminate him, he was soon killed under mysterious circumstances.

These five stories are typical of the type of rogue which milled around the bar and the relationship of their activity to the general atmosphere prevailing in the Middle East. With the exception of the Armenian antiques dealer, our protagonists used political acumen to make money, either directly or, as with the case of Intra, indirectly, by eliminating the opposition. Without exception, our players were highly sophisticated people, sensitive to their surroundings and believers in the art of the possible. They truly reflect the way things happened.

'How did you arrive at this idea? It is all-encompassing: it is the story of a bar, a hotel, a country, a whole region and how the world behaved towards them. Get going, show me some examples of what went on there.'

Riyad N. Al Rayyes, publisher

'Some of the things which took place in the bar cannot be told in a book, unless you have a death wish. Save them for another time, wait ten more years, then speak out.'

My father, Abu Saïd

12

BETWEEN THE PRINCE
AND
THE PRIME MINISTER

To outsiders, the ups and downs, the swift elevation and equally sudden collapse, of peoples and their careers in places where both society and governmental systems are in painful transition is a mystery. But in the Middle East that is the way things are and will continue to be until self-perpetuating systems with direction and continuity evolve and replace the suspect whims of the present governing classes.

In 1959, the large reception hall of the St George Hotel was the scene of a press conference held by visiting Jordanian Prime Minister Haza' Majali, a descendant of an old Jordanian family and a gentleman of exceptional wit and charm. The bar press was all there, but Majali, whose English was far from perfect, was having difficulty because his press aide was not present.

On seeing me in the front row of the reporters, Majali, in Arabic, asked me to help him with the conference and said he would give me an exclusive interview later. I switched hats and became Majali's translator. The press conference went well, to everyone's satisfaction – particularly the prime minister, who closed it by announcing 'Enough, my friend Saïd and I are going to have lunch now.'

We lunched at the grill room and as we were about to finish, Majali said, 'Saïd, I need you. Please, you must resign from Radio Free Europe and work for me. I want you in Washington; you will report to me directly.' He gave me no chance to answer, but added: 'Come to Amman next week, we'll settle everything then.'

I was twenty-four, committed to journalism and full of

doubt about King Hussein and his government. I did not want a government job, but I was complimented. I truly liked Majali's openness and bedouin elegance, and convinced myself that he would forget about his offer when back in Amman. There would be no need to offend him by refusing. Surprisingly, this didn't happen. His assistant telephoned from Jordan the following week, asking the date of my arrival. When he telephoned again, I gave him a date and began rehearsing my refusal speech, which contained many thanks for His Excellency's generosity and vote of confidence in my humble person.

The arrangements were made for a meeting at four o'clock one afternoon, but I arrived around noontime. With an hour to spare before my appointment, I decided to browse around Amman's main street, Wadi Seer, to see things, to feel the pulse of the town. A window display had drawn my attention, and I only become aware of a commotion about me belatedly and absently. An officer of the Arab Legion (as Jordan's army was then called) was shouting in my direction. There were other people nearby, so it did not immediately occur to me that the officer was addressing me.

But then the officer pointed a pistol at me and another officer covered me with a submachine gun. The senior officer, holding the pistol, ordered me to enter his car. I recognized him as the then Crown Prince Muhammed of Jordan, King Hussein's twenty-year-old brother. When I asked the Prince whether I had done anything wrong, I was told to keep quiet. When I said I was sorry if I had done anything wrong, the crown prince merely pointed his gun at my head and barked, '*Kaman kilmah we batayer dmaghek* (one more word and I'll blow your brains out).'

Moving swiftly, the car soon reached Zahran Palace, where Queen Mother Zein, King Hussein's and the prince's mother, lives. The prince jumped out, gun still in hand, and called for an officer in a shrill agitated voice. When he arrived the prince snapped: 'Take this man and discipline him. He is insolent.' No more was said. The prince disappeared, and the officer motioned me to follow him. I did. He deposited me at a tent of the palace guards. I asked to telephone the prime minister, with whom, I told the officer, I had an appointment. 'We don't have a telephone here,' the officer said.

'But I saw one in the other tent,' I insisted.

He snapped: 'I am not going to let you telephone the prime minister. My orders are clear.' I asked why I was being held. 'You will soon see,' the officer smirked in reply. He took off his palace guard's beret and began to undo his brass-buckled belt.

'You are not going to use that belt on me, are you?'

'I certainly am,' he replied, turning his back to me.

'Look here,' I said, 'I have a bad back and can't take punishment. If you hit me with that belt, I'll hit you back.'

Unconsciously, I was shouting and trembling. Three lieutenants and a captain rushed into the tent. The captain recognized me immediately. He ordered his junior colleagues out. 'Weren't you here two months ago to see His Majesty?' he enquired. 'You are a journalist, aren't you?'

'Yes, I had an interview with him. We talked about restoring political freedom,' I said cynically.

'I am very sorry,' he said. 'Please forget all this.' The captain was very nervous; he was calculating the consequences.

'I want to know what this is all about. What did I do? I was walking down the street by myself . . .'

'His Highness is a very nervous fellow,' the captain said. 'You probably did not applaud him when he passed through the street. He has a thing against people who don't applaud him.'

'Next time I'll know better,' I said. 'Can somebody take me to the prime minister's office?'

'I will.'

I reached Majali's office at four-twenty, after listening to fifteen minutes of argument as to why the incident was best forgotten. Majali, always an amiable man, met me at the door. After ordering two cups of Turkish coffee, he confidently turned to me, 'When do you want to start?'

'Can you tell me, sir, if an officer in the palace guards is more important than the prime minister?'

'What do you mean?' Majali asked, obviously irritated. So I told Majali the whole story. Majali's only reaction was: 'I did notice you were a little pale when you came in. You are lucky. Others get a whipping and possibly a few broken ribs.'

I asked: 'Why don't you have the king stop him?'

Majali lamented: 'Nobody can speak to the king about his family.'

'I will if you let me.'

'I won't let you.'

'What if Muhammed becomes king?' I asked.

He said: 'I would rather not think about it. I also would like to see you leave for Beirut and forget all about what happened today – everything.'

'Good day, Mr Prime Minister.'

'Goodbye, Saïd.'

Back at the Amman Club Hotel, I started a quick investigation of Muhammed's affairs and everyone I talked to had a bizarre tale to tell. A day after, I left Amman for Beirut. Upon arrival in Beirut, I started writing a story about my encounter with Prince Muhammed. While writing my story, the telephone rang. It was Amman, my friend, Majali's aide. 'Saïd, what are you doing?' he asked.

I said: 'I am writing a story.'

'About us?'

'Yes.'

'Listen, Saïd, don't be foolish. I am authorized to give what you want. Don't write the story.'

'What will you give?'

'Four hundred dinars [one thousand dollars], perhaps more.'

'Wonderful,' I said. 'I'll include your offer in my story.'

Amman pleaded: 'Don't do that. You have family here – they will suffer if you write the story.'

I said: 'My family has nothing to do with this. You can't frighten me.'

'Whether they have anything to do with your proposed foolishnesses or not is irrelevant. They would go to jail all the same.'

'You can't blackmail me,' I said.

He threatened: 'You would also lose your Jordanian pass-port.'

'You can't do this to people,' I said. 'You are mad.'

'Who do you work for?'

'I write for RFE and other people as well.'

'We can't let you send this to any paper that's sold in the Middle East,' my friend declared. 'However, you can send it to any paper that's not on sale here . . . We don't want a scandal.'

'Is that a bargain?' I asked.

'Yes', he said, adding, 'Goodbye. Think it over carefully.'

Thinking of my uncles, a non-political group of nice people, I knew what my choice had to be. The story could not be told in the Middle East. But I felt that it should be told in the US or another faraway place where it would not generate much fuss.

My unscheduled encounter with Prince Muhammed was not a Radio Free Europe type of story, so I sent it to my friends at *Newsday* of Long Island, happy with the thought that this was the end of the affair. *Newsday* was very pleased with the story, and featured it with the title 'Reporter Meets Prince – At Gun Point', paying me twice the going rate. But a friend of King Hussein of Jordan read it, became angry and sent a copy of the article to His Majesty.

Hussein and his prime minister had a meeting over the article during which Majali complained bitterly and without restraint about the behaviour of the crown prince. As expected, Hussein defended his brother and, without evidence, insisted that there was more to it than reported, that I must have made a rude gesture in the direction of the prince. Naturally, Hussein's opinion was what mattered.

The bar thus became a propaganda battleground between myself and the Jordanian palace. I began giving my colleagues stories about the corruption of Hussein's government, including his friends' involvement in hashish smuggling and gun-running. The Jordanians countered with inconsistent accusations which included spying, homosexuality and, eventually, pimping. Because members of the bar press were my friends and the Jordanian allegations were plainly stupid, I was winning. I was damaging them, while they did not affect me.

Two weeks later, His Highness's unchecked behaviour gave me total victory. Driving under the influence of alcohol very early one Friday morning, he refused to slow down to accommodate a crowd leaving a mosque after morning prayer and fatally injured one of them. When the worshippers turned into an angry mob and threatened his car, he pulled out a submachine gun and opened fire, killing three more of them and injuring many others. This was a big story and the bar press began looking into the sordid background of Prince Muhammed. Stories about him were carried by newspapers and wire services, but the most stinging indictment appeared in *Time* magazine.

Nonetheless, the attempt to absolve Muhammed continued. King Hussein wrote a letter to the editors of *Time* which was printed in the magazine. He denied all the charges against his brother and complained about the existence of a 'gutter press'. John Fistere began to promise bar journalists exclusive interviews with His Majesty in return for their silence and *Time* correspondent Denis Fodor was banned from entering Jordan because he had written the original anti-Muhammed story. As this was deemed to cripple his effectiveness, Fodor was withdrawn from Beirut and eventually pressured into resigning, one of the more shameful episodes in the editorial history of *Time*.

My own personal problems perpetuated themselves. The more the Jordanians tried to silence me through threats and one offer of a bribe, the more determined I became to focus attention on the danger inherent in having Prince Muhammed one heartbeat from the throne. Also, I could not help thinking about the cocked gun pointed at my head. Eventually, the Jordanians sent a special emissary to the bar to talk to my father. The man, a colonel in dark glasses, did not come for a discussion. He issued an ultimatum: either I leave Beirut in three weeks or I was as good as dead.

There was good reason to take the threat seriously. Strange characters with intimidating bulges under their jackets began appearing at the bar. One evening an inept chaser followed me to no less than five restaurants and bars before I lost him. My knowledgeable father advised me to leave Beirut, 'at least for a year'. More telling, CIA agent James Barracks, either as an act of friendship or because his bosses decided I was damaging Hussein's reputation, told me to leave because 'They've become preoccupied with eliminating you.'

I left Beirut for New York with thirty dollars in my pocket, and no idea how long I would be away or what I would do there. I never returned. Four years later, a royal decree issued in Amman announced the removal of Prince Muhammed as crown prince in favour of his younger brother Prince Hassan. No reasons were given.

With Muhammed's removal, the cycle was complete. The whole story demonstrates superbly the fickle nature of Middle Eastern politics. I moved from being a prime minister's favourite to an enemy of the régime of which he was an important part in a single afternoon for reasons which I invite the reader to judge.

The history of the bar includes a long list of former Middle Eastern ministers, generals and courtiers who lost favour overnight for unintelligible reasons, lonely, forlorn figures sitting in the corner of the bar whose positions of power disappeared suddenly, perhaps because they rejected a king's wish to sleep with their wives or refused a prime minister's order to hire an incompetent relative or declined to accompany a prince to a whorehouse.

13

STRANGE BEDFELLOWS

Intelligence organizations at times generate their own momentum and undertake activity contradictory to their countries' stated foreign policies. As with the 'Irangate' incident, we only hear about such matters when they go grossly wrong and democratic governments are obliged to explain contradictions. That the spies of the bar conducted 'their own foreign policy' is particularly true of the American CIA, and one of the earliest bar espionage stories demonstrates just how far afield agents can go: in this case, the CIA and the Palestinians cooperated against a then solidly pro-Western Iraq and the British in violation of the declared US foreign policy of common Anglo-American attitudes towards the Middle East.

This episode occurred at a time when US policy in the region was more receptive to the emergence of new régimes and rulers and supported moves towards democratic rule. British policy, on the other hand, advocated continued reliance on traditional leaders, sheikhs and kings, because they considered the Arabs incapable of self-rule. A wide divide in fact separated the two friendly powers and it showed more through their intelligence activities than in other respects.

Certain elements in this story of Anglo-American friction have never been told before. Because revelation of the details of this incident could have adverse consequences or endanger the lives of some of the participants, I have eliminated the names of the Syrian officers involved, used an acronym for the leading player and refrained from specifying the time of the incident.

The short, stocky man who walked into the bar was dishevelled and in need of a shave, obviously out of place.

Before any of the waiters could ask him to leave, his nervous eyes settled on Abu Saïd (Mohamad Nimr Audeh, not to be confused with Abu Saïd Aburish) who, though with some friends, responded to Ali Bitar's signal and walked over to meet the intruder. Abu Saïd had not recognized him, but as they went into the lobby the man identified himself. The two stopped and embraced, Arab-style, to seal their fond remembrance of each other.

M.S.N. was Iraqi, a former officer of the Liberation Army, the all-Arab volunteer force sent to Palestine by the Arab League in 1948 to help fight the Jews and stop the creation of Israel. M.S.N. had fought bravely in the Jerusalem area, at one point thwarting an Israeli attack which would have surrounded the city. He thus had become a news-maker and met Abu Saïd, then working for the London *Daily Mail*.

M.S.N. had a strange tale to tell. He had come to Beirut from Damascus on a phoney passport, had no place to go and had remembered his old Jerusalem friend who, people told him, was always in the bar. M.S.N. had been sent to Damascus by Iraqi Prime Minister Nuri Saïd to assassinate the President of Syria, but decided to defect instead. Before the man had finished his story, Abu Saïd hurried him away from the hotel, collecting his small suitcase from the door-man, and took him to his own house. He barely took the time to warn Ali Bitar and the doorman not to tell anyone about his visitor.

Over endless cups of Turkish coffee, M.S.N. continued his story. He had been told by the people who hired him as a gunman that there would be no consequences to the assassination in terms of his personal safety. If, after shooting the president, he managed to escape and return to Iraq, so be it; otherwise he should surrender because the death of the Syrian president would be followed by an assumption of power in Syria by army officers friendly to Iraq who would eventually free him. The planned assassination was a first step in a plot to take over the Syrian government and replace it by one friendly to Iraq.

At the time, Iraq was staunchly pro-British. One of Iraq's

aims, with British connivance, was to annexe Syria and merge it with Iraq to create a pro-British country of nineteen million people. In view of most Syrians' opposition to this plan, internal subversion was the first step towards such an eventuality. The British policy was clear and simple: to support the schemes of the Iraqi government, then ruled by the pro-British Hashemite monarchy, and thereby enhance British regional influence. They reasoned that the monarchy would bring much-needed stability to Syria and the whole operation would strike a blow against the inherent Syrian radicalism which was threatening to infect other countries.

The Americans saw things differently: their instincts favoured a republican Syria with democratic pretensions, but a country of fifteen million people posed a greater threat to Israel than a bunch of fragmented Arab states constantly at each others' throats. Besides, the US frowned on the British desire to perpetuate their influence and wanted to replace Britain as the dominant power in the area.

American opposition to British-Iraqi plans for Syria had an unlikely ally in Haj Amin Al Husseini, the mufti of Jerusalem and chairman of the Arab Higher Committee, the organization which claimed to represent the Palestinians and the precursor of today's PLO. The mufti's opposition to an Iraqi-Syrian union had deep roots: he hated the conservative rulers of Iraq and the idea of a strong country under their leadership because they would preempt him as Palestinian spokesman, perhaps would deal with Israel over his head, sue for peace. The PLO remains wary of such a union for the very same reasons.

Abu Saïd was aware that M.S.N.'s story was too sensitive to be used in a news story. Among other things, he feared what the Iraqis might do if he, Abu Saïd, exposed them. A committed Palestinian and long-time follower of the mufti, Abu Saïd shared his ideals and felt an obligation to apprise the mufti of his God-sent discovery.

On Abu Saïd's instructions, M.S.N. wrote a lengthy report detailing his adventures as an assassin for hire. He had been paid a lot of money and promised more, but what had appealed to him most was reinstatement as an officer in the Iraqi army, the position he had resigned to join the Liberation army and fight for Palestine.

M.S.N.'s report ignored the most obvious question: why he did not go through with the assassination. After a thorough interrogation, Abu Saïd determined that in spite of this omission M.S.N. was telling the truth. The omission was no more than a reluctance to admit that he had 'chickened out'. Also, the lack of pro-Iraqi developments in Syria could be attributed to confusion in the wake of M.S.N.'s disappearance.

The report was forwarded to the mufti in Cairo by his cousin, confidante and representative in Beirut, Haidar Al Husseini. Abu Saïd needed an immediate answer about what to do because M.S.N. was becoming moody and unhappy in his captivity, and his heavy consumption of whisky was beginning to alarm his host.

After Cairo responded, there was a three-way meeting involving Haidar Al Husseini (Haj Amin's nephew and son-in-law), Abu Saïd and M.S.N. in which Haidar satisfied himself as to the authenticity of the information. Then Haidar told a shocked Abu Saïd what to do: 'Find a way to get this information to the Americans as soon as possible.' They discussed how to do it; Abu Saïd counselled M.S.N. that a solution was on the way and returned to the bar.

A lot of the American bar operatives would have loved to lay their hands on what Abu Saïd possessed but, aware of the value of M.S.N.'s disclosures, Abu Saïd held out until Archie Roosevelt, then the CIA station chief, came to the bar in person. The two knew each other superficially. At Abu Saïd's request, a whispering session took place in a corner of the bar.

The polite, highly polished grandson of Teddy Roosevelt and an accomplished Orientalist, Roosevelt listened attentively as Abu Saïd recited the M.S.N. saga. At the end, he stared Abu Saïd straight in the eyes and asked why he was being favoured with such valuable information. In the end, Abu Saïd came clean. The mufti and the CIA had a common interest: to stop British-Iraqi plans. A smiling Archie Roosevelt nodded agreement and disappeared towards the US Embassy.

Roosevelt's first and only known move was to contact CIA agent Miles Copeland in Damascus, instructing him to stop his search for the would-be assassin, who was alive and mopey and drinking Abu Saïd out of house and home. Copeland, like Roosevelt, had been acting on a CIA tip from Baghdad that an assassin was in Damascus. So long as he was still at large, the CIA would continue to fear for the life of the Syrian president. Copeland told the president, who just happened to be a friend of his, that part of the plot had been uncovered and that the telephone numbers, code names and other details of the army officers in league with Iraq would be provided in due course.

The mufti was extremely pleased with Abu Saïd's performance, and I have no doubt that Roosevelt's bosses were happy with him.

In this chapter in the secret war between the CIA and Britain to control Syria, the CIA had been so desperate to locate the would-be assassin that they were willing to pay for the information. Years later, Miles Copeland told Abu Saïd he should have asked Roosevelt for 'a fortune'. Not only did Roosevelt and Copeland discover M.S.N. but, thinking the CIA had masterminded the defection, Iraq lived in constant awe of its power and ability and never again tried anything as blatant.

The finale of this story is as strange as its beginning. The chief of Lebanese security, Farid Chehab, made a rare appearance at the bar and extended an 'invitation' to Abu Saïd to visit him. When the two men met, Chehab advised Abu Saïd to get rid 'of the gunman. The Syrians know where he is and they are likely to come for him. I leave it to you as to how to do it.'

Abu Saïd himself was getting nervous about what to do with his ward. M.S.N. had convinced Haidar Al Husseini and, through him, the mufti that his actions were more deliberate than they had appeared at first, that he was an

152

idealogue committed to their way in opposition to Britain and Iraq. As a result, they were trying to organize a passport so that he could go to Pakistan and help instruct some of the mufti's followers who were using that country as a training camp for operations not too dissimilar from the one that brought him to their attention.

Two problems faced Abu Saïd simultaneously: his group was taking its time providing the false passport and he could not be sure that it would be good enough to guarantee M.S.N.'s safety. The man had, after all, trusted him personally. After another bar meeting with Roosevelt, the CIA provided a passport and funds for M.S.N. to proceed to Pakistan. Abu Saïd informed Haidar Al Husseini and the mufti, both of whom were thankful for the CIA's generosity and cooperation.

M.S.N. worked for the mufti in Pakistan for six long years. It is highly doubtful that he ever knew that he was a small pawn in a complex game beyond his understanding; he thought the passport and the money came from the mufti. He returned to Iraq only after a change of government there, and has given up his life of excitement in favour of running a small nightclub.

What would have happened had this contact and many other US PLO contacts been exposed is anyone's guess. What would have happened had Roosevelt been misled and his failure uncovered is even more disturbing to contemplate. Perhaps it would have led to another Congressional hearing aimed at curbing 'unauthorized' CIA activity. Conversely, many of the mufti's followers would have been shocked by their leader's cooperation with the CIA against fellow Arabs, no matter what the reason. As Archie himself says in his recent book, *For Lust of Knowing*, success has a thousand fathers but failure is an orphan.

The field confrontation between the CIA and the British is no less intriguing. Was this part of US policy or was the CIA acting on its own? To what extent did these differences of opinion contribute towards destabilizing the Middle East? Was Suez but one example of this strife and did the secret

153

wars between the US and the UK to control the Middle East contribute to the downfall of the monarchy in Iraq and the Shah in Iran?

Even today, there are no easy answers to those questions. What is clear is that the bar was a place where a would-be assassin, entrusted with a job aimed at changing the map of the Middle East, sought refuge, and where American and Palestinian policies found common ground at the expense of the British and their Arab allies.

14

CARELESS EDEN?
SCEPTICAL NASSER

The tense atmosphere generated by the 1956 Suez crisis enveloped the Middle East in a way that is unlikely to be witnessed again. It was the first time a Middle Eastern country openly confronted the major powers, a significant historic event which unleashed the pent-up passions of the area's people and signalled the end of colonialism.

Beirut was consumed by the nationalistic flames raging throughout the Arab world. The man in the street was solidly pro-Nasser, supporting his nationalization of the Suez Canal and defiance of Britain and France. Most Arab leaders firmly backed Nasser and King Hussein, then a boy of twenty-one, had appointed a pro-Nasser government, promising the Egyptian leader his unqualified support.

The bar press was divided as never before or since. American journalists openly criticized their country's allies and were full of derision for old-fashioned gunboat diplomacy, while British and French correspondents reverted to an immovable colonial stance, their basic nationalistic feelings overwhelming their doubts about their countries' policies. A new set of visitors began coming to the bar, what might be called crisis-watchers, among them a number of diplomats who found the bar a better source of information than their embassies. One of these diplomats was A.R.S., the Jordanian chargé d'affaires in Beirut.

Another new bar regular at the time was E.M., the highest-ranking Arab employee of the British Embassy in Beirut, an engaging Lebanese man-about-town who, sensitive to the anti-British atmosphere generated by the crisis, took to drinking alone while furtively eyeing the various groups engaged in intense conversation. E.M. had paid special attention to the agitated Jordanian chargé and after a watch of three days managed to intercept him on his way out of the bar and engage him in brief, unsuspicious conversation.

The result of this exchange was a meeting between the Jordanian chargé and E.M. which took place the following day at Shallal Intalias, a small resort village a few miles north of Beirut. The British Embassy employee wasted no time. He offered to sell Jordan a bundle of British Embassy documents which proved the existence of plans to invade Suez, clear instructions to the embassy of what was to be done the moment hostilities commenced and an indication of when and how they would begin. The asking price was one hundred thousand dollars, one-quarter of which was to be paid the moment the Jordanian agreed to the deal and the documents were delivered, the rest after the contents were verified. For the time being, the seller limited himself to telling how a safe was accidently left open long enough for him to steal the documents.

A hundred thousand dollars was a lot of money in 1956, and Jordan in particular was not a big spender in the area of espionage. Any decision to proceed with the deal would have to come from the very top, from Hussein himself. With this in mind, the Jordanian requested and obtained a delay of forty-eight hours before giving a final answer.

Before consulting with his government, the Jordanian returned to the bar to check on the character of the dapper Lebanese. The information he obtained told of a polite man who kept to himself, but beyond his connection with the British Embassy little was known about him. The most important element was that he had a clean record; there was no history of his trying to sell anything to anyone.

In Amman, King Hussein saw in this a God-sent intelligence coup which might confirm his credentials as a staunch supporter of Nasser and eliminate any lingering doubts about his willingness to oppose his one-time friend, Britain. He instructed his man in Beirut to go ahead with the deal and volunteered to pay for the documents from 'special funds'. Another meeting at Shallal Intalias was organized and the first payment and the documents were exchanged, to be followed by a visit to Jordan by E.M. after the documents had been checked and verified.

Jordanian intelligence officers told an excited Hussein that the documents were genuine; the wording, seal and signatures were judged to be authentic. A beaming Hussein entrusted the papers with a cover note to his chef de cabinet and dispatched him to Cairo for a meeting with Nasser. The handwritten cover note told Nasser that, now that war was on the way, he, Hussein, was ready to fight with him.

E.M. arrived in Amman to collect the rest of his money the day Hussein's downcast chef de cabinet returned from Cairo. Nasser had examined the documents with his own intelligence chiefs, but had decided they were fakes, aimed at frightening Egypt into making concessions in the face of British and French threats. He had thanked the Jordanian emissary and had spoken of a clumsy British attempt to undermine his confidence. When the Jordanian emissary had protested, Nasser cast doubt on the honesty of the informer and, citing their deposit in a Beirut diplomatic post, insisted that the documents 'were too good to be true'.

Hussein sided with Nasser; he summoned his intelligence officers, scolded them for being unsuspecting fools and praised Nasser's clearness of vision. On being told that the informer was in town to collect the rest of the money, Hussein ordered his arrest pending a thorough investigation; he wanted to retrieve the first payment. A shouting, protesting E.M. was collected from his hotel, thrown into a Jordanian jail, committed to solitary confinement and subjected to gruelling interrogations.

Two weeks later, Israel launched its surprise attack on Egypt, which was followed by an Anglo-French ultimatum to stay clear of the strategic waterway and by the landing of these countries' troops along the Suez Canal. The day after the Israeli attack and before the Anglo-French landing, John Mecklin of *Time* magazine was interviewing Hussein when Nasser came on the telephone and advised Hussein in the strongest possible terms against joining the battle.

According to those at the Hussein-Mecklin meeting, Nasser pleaded with Hussein to stay out because 'It's a coordinated joint effort – the British and French will attack soon – all you'd do is have your army destroyed. Your information was correct.' The Anglo-French moves which followed appeared to confirm the Nasser claim; they were in line with the information contained in E.M.'s stolen documents.

E.M. was soon released from jail and returned to Beirut, outwardly a little chastened and wiser for the experience. His appearances at the bar were the same as they had been before his contact with the Jordanian diplomat. But the story did not stop there.

A few weeks after the shooting at Suez had stopped and while the whole world joined in a heated debate about the existence of a tripartite conspiracy against Egypt, the Beirut daily *Al Youm* ran a story about strange happenings within the British Embassy in Beirut. The *Al Youm* story, confirmed by other publications, told of the firing of seven Lebanese employees of the embassy on suspicion of stealing classified documents. The embassy, the story added, had offered a huge reward of one hundred thousand Lebanese lira (thirty thousand dollars) for the return of the missing documents. This intriguing development caused considerable discussion among the bar press but died a natural death without anyone determining the nature of the missing documents. The British Embassy refused to comment.

E.M. was not fired and not even investigated. He retired from his job at the British Embassy in the late sixties and continues to draw a pension from Her Majesty's government.

This is a most intriguing tale. The Jordanian and Egyptian parts of this story are known, but very little is known about the British aspect and E.M. himself has refused to discuss it, not even with his original Jordanian contact. Two former British Intelligence officers who operated in the Middle East and would have had reason to know about this story refused to comment.

It may be that Nasser's original instincts were correct. The money E.M. had requested was substantial, but he came from an old monied family, he was not in need and his initial contact with the Jordanian at the bar was too obvious, even taking into consideration the pressures of time and the need to sell the documents in a hurry. There is no explanation as to how E.M. justified his absence in Jordan, nor for his escaping the embassy firings, which must have involved a thorough investigation of everyone there.

The dismissal of the other British Embassy employees could be explained in terms of fear for E.M.'s position after his mission failed, an attempt to absolve him by confirming that the documents had been stolen – after all, there is good reason to believe he was important to the embassy.

Nasser's original misgivings were sound; reported activities at the British Embassy in Beirut confirm this. Nasser's later declarations to Hussein cannot be dismissed as an attempt to dissuade the king from hasty action. The mere existence of the documents at the embassy in Beirut, the way they reached Hussein and E.M.'s survival can be explained only in terms of an attempt to frighten Nasser or to undermine Eden, or both. Clearly a British political or intelligence group had serious misgivings about Eden's Suez adventure.

The real way the Suez invasion information was obtained and its purpose remains a mystery, but there is no doubt about a serious lapse in security which occurred at the American Embassy in the early fifties, an outright act of stupidity by the local CIA station chief.

One of the first CIA officers to operate out of Beirut was George Britt, who had been an OSS officer during the Second World War and who was a gentleman of the old school with a deep belief in human sympathy – the opposite of the hyperactive espionage operatives of legend. He saw his work as an American crusade to save the world and to introduce new humanitarian values to parts of the world that had suffered the old-fashioned colonialism of Britain and France.

Among the many things that reflected George's attitude was a commitment to hiring people from downtrodden minority groups. In Beirut this meant Armenians and

Palestinians. So when the US Embassy organized its first CIA station in the city and needed a wireless operator to transmit its intelligence data, George sought a member of one of these two minorities to fill the job. After a brief search, he located H.S., a twenty-one-year-old Palestinian who had been trained at a civilian wireless school in Cairo and who met the requirements in more ways than one: his technical expertise was the best available and his family had been displaced during the 1948 Arab-Israeli War. A pleased George offered H.S. the job, which was readily accepted.

In reality, the unsophisticated H.S. had no idea what he was transmitting or receiving and there was no way he could because everything was encoded. More often than not, George or someone else would look over his shoulder while he performed his tedious work. His bosses were happy with his performance, while he enjoyed the benefits of a salary which was higher than what was paid his equals in education.

The one element neither employer or employee had counted on was H.S.'s father, a radical Palestinian follower of the mufti of Jerusalem, the Arafat of his days. The father, a more cunning man than the innocent Morse machine operator, decided that what his son was doing might be of value to his leader, the mufti. He quizzed his son mercilessly about his work, but got nowhere because the young man had nothing to reveal. Besides, he liked George and his job, and did not want to endanger his position.

When George was transferred back to the US for eventual retirement, he was replaced by a man who was not so friendly to H.S. and who was in addition quite demanding. H.S.'s growing resentment of his new boss, who was not clever enough to keep an eye on him, led him to write down some of the coded messages he had transmitted and give them to his father, who took them to the mufti's Beirut office.

For two months H.S. kept the mufti supplied with copies of American intelligence reports originating in Beirut, but the mufti's people were unable to break the American code. The whole affair eventually died a natural death of neglect because the mufti's men convinced their chief that the messages contained nothing; the Americans would never trust a dim-witted kid with valuable information.

Months later, H.S.'s father became seriously ill and the son who adored him wanted to provide a level of medical care which his own salary could not cover. His father's attitude and the whisperings which accompanied the delivery of some of the coded messages to his hand finally convinced him that he was dealing with something quite valuable, something which was worth a lot of money to someone. Having heard some stories about the St George Hotel bar, H.S. decided that what was available to him could have a ready market there. After all, his friend George had been a bar regular, and so was his new boss.

Equipped with copies of a week's worth of reports, he marched to the hotel to try his luck. Too afraid to enter the lair of sophistication and high life, he only managed to engage the doorman in friendly conversation. The doorman remembers an awkward young man who shuffled his feet and spoke haltingly. He finally managed to tell the doorman what he did and his reason for being there.

To the knowing eye of the doorman, H.S. was too naive and nervous to be a con man. Perhaps, thought the doorman, just perhaps H.S. was telling the truth, in which case he felt an obligation to tell someone who would care, preferably an American with embassy connections. He told H.S. to return the following day while he worked out a plan of action.

That evening, the doorman apologetically stopped J.E. and asked if he could have a word. Hat in hand, but closer to J.E. than he had ever been, the doorman whispered all he had heard from the young man, including his name. J.E. headed for the bar after promising an answer early the following day. J.E.'s colleague, who was waiting for him at the bar, provided half the answer by confirming that there was 'an Arab' wireless operator.

The following day, J.E. was conferring with the doorman at ten-thirty a.m. Would he please buy everything from H.S. for fifty dollars after ascertaining that no copies had been made and that H.S. had not contacted anyone else. He gave the doorman a hundred dollars, fifty for each of them.

H.S. accepted the money, a small fortune in those days, and handed over his bundle of coded messages. J.E., who was sitting in a car across the street, walked over and relieved the doorman of the papers before he could contemplate doing anything with them. H.S. was summarily fired from his job upon his return to the embassy. Though no reason was given, he received substantial severance pay. He could not be prosecuted because he was not a US citizen and the embassy had no jurisdiction over him. Besides, the likelihood was that the Americans were trying to contain the incident rather than publicize it. Any repercussions within the embassy and the CIA remain unknown. H.S.'s careless new boss died soon after from a heart attack. J.E. was in Beirut for years, a bar regular who always took time out for a friendly greeting to his friend the doorman.

What both these stories demonstrate is the reputation the bar enjoyed as a centre for anyone with important things to say or sell. Whether E.M. was acting on his own or with the connivance of British Intelligence is secondary to the fact that the bar is the place he used for the effort. Even a slow-witted young man recognized it as as the place where he could flog his bundle of secrets.

15
GREEN WITH MONEY

As spies go, James Russell Barracks was very odd indeed. Everything about him contradicted what you might imagine a spy should be. At six feet four inches and about one hundred and seventy pounds he was noticeably tall and thin – qualities accentuated by his beautifully tailored suits. He had thinning brown hair, unusually big ears and the annoying habit of rolling his lips against each other to keep them wet. He walked with unusually long, fast strides, suggesting that something important was afoot. Unfailingly, he took time out for a loud hello to people in the St George Hotel lobby and bar. Barracks wanted to be noticed and he was, though the ensuing gossip about him went beyond the obvious.

Barracks was a homosexual at a time when the CIA considered such people a security risk. Legend has it that he had been fired because of his homosexuality, but was reinstated after he proceeded to scoop local spies in Beirut and other Middle East spots by freely reporting pieces of important intelligence well ahead of them, thus making himself indispensable. The one aspect of Barracks' character which appeared to fit the mould was his imperturbability, for he kept whatever pressures went with the job well under control, submerged beneath his chattiness and ready, if over-done, smile.

I could tell that the Barracks who approached me as I sat at one of the tables of the St George Hotel bar one sunny day in April 1960 was agitated because his smile and his hello to bar regulars were both absent. He came directly towards me, pulled a chair aside and sat down while ordering a dry martini cocktail and inquiring if I wanted another drink.

At his suggestion we moved to a table on the terrace so

we could talk privately. Without preamble Barracks told me that he had received a message, coded and unclear, concerning one of the two people arrested in Beirut two weeks before for exchanging six hundred thousand dollars of Cuban currency on the open market. Barracks thought one had to be a CIA agent who must be got out. Barracks claimed, and subsequent events support his claim, that he did not know which of the two was the CIA agent but that something about 'going home' would be mentioned during a preliminary hearing in a Lebanese court scheduled for later that week.

Calling on my personal loyalty as a friend, Barracks asked if I could 'handle things' for him because he was leaving for Washington the following morning for a period of at least a week. He needed a journalist so the involvement would look natural. Yes, bribing the police to fix the evidence and possibly the judge himself would be expensive and of course there was no way of predetermining what the outcome would be. The envelope he gave me contained five thousand Lebanese pounds as well as the telephone number of a man who would give me more money if I needed it, though the paymaster was not to know anything else. My acceptance of the unwelcome assignment lifted Barracks' uncharacteristic gloom only partially; he left the bar, still dispensing his usual effusive goodbyes and leaving me to face about half a dozen pairs of staring, inquisitive eyes.

My initial inquiries about the case entailed telephoning some Lebanese journalist friends who had all heard about it, but who described it as a small-time smuggling operation involving a couple: a Belgian-born woman called Nicole Cuvellier and an American called John Green. They were accused of exchanging Cuban pesos which did not belong to them. The only useful piece of information I was able to obtain came from my photographer friend, Harry Kondakjian, who gave me the date of the hearing in return for a commission to work with me as the photographer on the story. I agreed, so it would all look journalistic and above board.

Harry and I and a perennial court watcher sat in the old

court room as the only audience of the hearing. We were soon followed by Cuvellier and Green, who were instructed to sit on the front benches reserved for plaintiffs. Green looked all-American, middle-aged and tired, in a badly cut, almost shapeless, American-tailored light summer suit. He was constantly running his hand through his grey hair. Cuvellier was something else, an elegant lady in a blue shantung silk suit and matching hat, the hard blueness of which broken by a beautiful gold pin with a diamond in the middle. She had an elfin, totally gaelic face, small dimples, deep red-coloured hair and sparkling green eyes which shone a long distance. She dressed to overcome her five-feet-two-inch frame and succeeded; her smile exposed a perfect set of teeth. She had walked in, handbag held firmly in the elegant fingers of her left hand, taking sturdy, firm steps. It was a study in contrast; the lady had it all.

My contemplation of Cuvellier and Green came to an end when the judge walked into the courtroom unannounced, forcing us to stand up in a hurry. The judge nodded permission to sit down and began to read out a prepared statement. It amounted to an announcement that certain facts revealed by a new police report suggested that the case was more complex than originally thought. The judge was not sure that his court was the proper tribunal for the case; possibly a higher court was needed. Pending that decision, the judge ordered both Cuvellier and Green to be remanded in custody on a bail of twenty-five thousand Lebanese lira each while the question of the court of jurisdiction was decided. Meanwhile, he asked both of them, in French, how they pleaded.

Green pleaded innocent. Cuvellier pleaded innocent as well, but her plea contained what I wanted to hear: she told the judge she wanted 'to go home'. No doubt about it – my job was to help Cuvellier. I walked from the court preoccupied with the need for money to provide bail for Cuvellier. Harry Kondakjian ran out of court as if it had just caught fire.

Barracks' treasurer did not flinch when I telephoned him with the request for the bail money. I remember mentioning the reason for it and being struck by his lack of interest in anything except where I banked and my current account number.

The following day the money was in my account, and Harry's pictures of Cuvellier and Green were on the front pages of two Lebanese newspapers above short stories suggesting that espionage was suspected. Fuming at Harry's behaviour, I hurriedly posted the bail money and instructed my trusted taxi driver friend Abdu to take the papers to the women's jail, pick up Cuvellier and deposit her at the St George Hotel where instructions were given to put her in room 104, a first-floor room with a separate entrance which by now contained two bouquets of yellow roses.

I decided not to contact Cuvellier for a day or so, but to limit myself to watching her movements to determine whether others would try to reach her. The concierge and telephone operator agreed to help the monitoring efforts, which produced nothing.

Madame Cuvellier was to the manor born. Her first day of freedom saw her make a brief visit to the hairdresser, then the swimming pool where, sitting in a far corner by herself, she drank two Camparis and soda. Later she bought a pocket book, vanished to her room for about three hours and reappeared in time for an aperitif on the terrace. She had dinner alone at the grill room, then went back to her room by ten in the evening. Whatever she wore was perfect for the occasion; she shone even by the standards of the exceptionally elegant surroundings.

The following day I tried to establish direct contact with her. I called her from one of the hotel's telephone booths, asking to meet her because I had a message for her. She said she was busy and hung up. A few hours later I telephoned again and phrased my message more subtly, alluding to my responsibility for the St George Hotel arrangements, but that didn't go far either. I decided to wait one whole day while I thought of ways to reach 'the haughty bitch'.

After a sleepless night of analysis, I rushed to the St George Hotel in the morning, had the operator connect me with Cuvellier and hurriedly begged her not to hang up because all I wanted was 'to get you home'. The response was immediate; it worked. She came down the stairs from room 104, gave me a very firm handshake, walked along with me to the bar and out to the small table just outside, the one Barracks and I used during our meeting.

The only people at the bar were two members of the Ten A.M. Club, Sam Brewer of the *New York Times* and Bill Eveland of the CIA. Sam was on his usual Gibson cocktail and Bill was drinking whisky, so I thought it in order to have a drink rather than coffee and Cuvellier joined me by ordering a Ricard.

It was an uneasy meeting. No, she did not need money but she wanted to go home promptly. Green would talk, particularly if he heard she was out. She did not know who Barracks was, and she was not keen on meeting him. To her, my job was to determine who the judge of whatever court was going to be, then bribe him to acquit her. She was sure someone would be in touch with me who knew more about her. There was a strong hint that having a novice like me handle her case offended her.

All this took one hour and two drinks. She was hard: the wrapping was beautiful, but she issued orders, used few words to make herself understood and automatically reduced me to a willing errand boy. With very little to offer, I settled for telling her that I'd call her the following day.

Another day and another drink at the bar, followed by the stares of the foreign press corps, who had by then read Cuvellier's story in a bulletin which translated local newspaper articles into English. Their attempts to interview her failed, though Arthur Cooke of the London *Daily Mail* wrote a highly speculative story which ran on the front page.

That day Cuvellier and I lunched at the grill room. We talked about everyday things, mostly Beirut, local wines and French influence in the Lebanon but not a single word about our common problem. Cuvellier, maintaining her elevated position, ordered the wine and signed the bill with a smile while making a statement that she'd pay her own expenses.

Our dining and wining routine was a wait for two things: the decision announcing the proper court and Barracks' return. News from Barracks came first; a message through his money handler told me that he was delayed in Washington for an undetermined period of time, but that I was to continue 'my good work'. Another transfer of funds was effected.

My relationship with Cuvellier changed as a result of a strange, small incident. Having decided to venture beyond the confines of the St George bar and grill room, we walked down the street west of the hotel on our way to a small shabby street full of restaurants, bars and nightclubs in search of something different. As we turned left on the first street north I instinctively put my hand under Cuvellier's elbow and moved her to the inside of the sidewalk with me on the outside. She smiled, genuinely for a change.

After we were seated in the Rumanian restaurant Cuvellier smiled again. 'You are a well-brought-up young man,' she said.

'Thank you. What brings this about?'

'The way you insist on walking on the outside in the street.'

'Oh! School manners, no more.'

'Where was college school?'

'A lovely place in Quaker, Pennsylvania.'

'I should have guessed; the gentle folk. How did you get into this?'

'I didn't get into anything. I am doing a friend a favour. How about you?'

'By accident. A long time ago . . .'

'Surely not that long ago . . .'

'So you are gallant as well.' And this time there was a laugh.

'I am sorry I am not what you appear to need, but I am trying.'

'No need for you to apologize. I just don't like what's happening.'

'Yes, more and more papers are chasing the story. They claim the Cuban currency you exchanged was about to be discontinued by Castro. Anything in it?'

'Everything. I knew Green would squeal. If only we'd exchanged the rest of the money!'

'What rest?'

'Two million dollars more.'

'Christ, that's a lot of money.'

'Yes, but you're better off not knowing more! Anyway, this restaurant was a good idea. The beef was good. Thank you very much.'

'Would you like to go anywhere else?'

'Yes. Take me dancing, please. I love to dance but no one has taken me dancing for years. How sad!'

'Okay. We'll go to the Cave du Rois – just down the street.'

The Cave du Rois was one of the poshest discos in the world. We drank, danced, discussed books and talked about each other until three in the morning. Not only was she a good dancer, she was an architect by education, an eleventh-generation graduate architect descendant of the famous Cuvellier who studied the subject to satisfy the family after a classical convent education. To her, *The Great Gatsby* was the only modern novel worth reading because it embodied America, man's new experience. She wanted to know about Arabic poetry, particularly of the pre-Islamic period because the emergence of Islam stifled the creative spirit; poets stopped being free after that.

For over a week Cuvellier and I forgot about who and where we were. We enjoyed each other's company the fresh, passionate way new lovers do and without rehearsal took to spending a lot of time at the bar to tease all the people who wondered about our relationship and wanted to get the inside story of the Cuvellier-Green Affair, the name given to the situation by the local press.

Suddenly Barracks was back, on cue to interrupt Cuvellier's attempts to change my ties and talk me into a permanent state of grey suits. Why didn't I know more about who the judge would be, he demanded? My handling of Harry Kondakjian was abysmal. What the hell was I doing spending money like a drunken sailor? To Barracks my job was to get Cuvellier out of Lebanon and 'not to offer her my young body as a consolation'. Barracks' anger was met with equal anger from me. After all, I was neither a CIA operative nor a messenger, simply a naive young reporter who needed the money.

The three-way meeting between Cuvellier, Barracks and myself was a study in the spy class system. I sat on the outside, ignored by both, while they were polite to each other to the point of nausea, though they disagreed sharply on everything. My superfluous presence was the result of Barracks' wish to have me continue as Cuvellier's companion.

Barracks wanted to know where the rest of the money, the Cuban and Lebanese currency they had, was, but she had no answer except that it might be with Green. He wanted to know why she aborted the mission, yet utterly rejected her reasoning that Green was endangering everything through his behaviour, his spending of five thousand dollars in one evening and his bragging, which made her opt to make it look like a smuggling operation. Finally, when Barracks lashed out, accusing her of ineptness for not having bribed her way out of the country immediately the police arrested her, she cynically answered that Lebanese jails and the lesbians in them appealed to her.

Having unsuccessfully tried to browbeat her, Barracks reverted to a cooler mood. He told her twenty-five thousand dollars were being deposited in her account in Switzerland and that he would be away again so she should stay in touch with me to provide the bar habitués 'with their vicarious pleasures'. As he left, Cuvellier, without any trace of emotion, almost inaudibly, looked at me and said, 'I don't like queer sons of beetches; they're veecious.'

Soon we discovered the background to Cuvellier-Green was thickening. Judge Dreize of the High Court was appointed to try the case. Barracks saw me one more time to tell me Dreize was 'easy' but that Green must be punished and that I should continue using his 'treasurer' in his absence. Simultaneously, Ali Bitar, then the head waiter in the bar, saw fit to warn me to be careful because 'they [the press corps] saw you with Barracks and they all think you're CIA. Please be careful.'

Dreize's cousin, a lawyer himself, was a bar habitué,

though a bit of an outsider with whom I had exchanged no more than a cursory greeting. I solicited Ali Bitar's help in arranging a meeting with him at the bar, which was done promptly. Maître Dreize, as he pompously called himself, knew my purpose and readily volunteered to act as go between with his cousin as well as act as Cuvellier's solicitor. He wanted ten thousand dollars for both of them in return for guaranteeing Cuvellier's acquittal, though he winced at a heavy sentence for Green. We agreed to 'cooperate'.

Finding a way to bribe the judge was easier than placating the Lebanese press. Bribing all of them into silence was morally possible but economically unfeasible. Besides, most Lebanese journalists would have taken the money and run to write the story to scandalize us. Additionally they derived extra mileage from a terse, communistically unimaginative announcement from Havana accusing 'imperialist agent Batista of having escaped the country with millions of dollars worth of pesos in cash which he is using to finance operations against the people's revolution. Said currency was being discontinued to strike against nefarious imperialist plots.'

'Imperialist plots' became the phrase of the week with the Lebanese press. Cuvellier-Green were part of an 'imperialist plot' to undermine Beirut's free market position, cried Beirut's newspapers, demanding the severest punishment for the perpetrators. The St George bar joke of the week, followed by giggles from all listeners, was that Saïd was in the middle of an 'imperialist plot', while one colleague described Cuvellier and me as the 'Chic and Sheikh Duo'.

Where was Barracks? It was late June, the date of the trial was set for early July, the noise level from the press was deafening, but Barracks was away. Was Cuvellier being set up? Was she being sacrificed for a reason neither of us knew? She must have suspected that but she never said anything. Meanwhile, the commandant of the internal security division showed up in person at the St George Hotel bar and invited me to visit him. I was summonsed.

Commandant 'Abdallah Dweiri' was short, fat, hairy, wore

civilian clothes and sweated profusely. June 1960 was a hot month so he did a lot of sweating in the spacious office in the Sûreté Building where he received me. He leaned over a big desk full of folders, resting both his elbows on it, picked up a dull letter opener with one hand, used it to clean the nails of the other hand and then used it to clean his teeth.

My filthy interrogator first wanted to know the nature of my relationship with Cuvellier and, when I said we were 'friends' and winked in a conspiratorial Arab style to suggest mischief, he still wasn't amused. Later I had to explain Radio Free Europe and everything about the bar including Maître Dreize, whom I described as a 'dear personal friend whom I loved'. Dweiri let me go after impounding my passport.

Two days after, Barracks, the old smiling happy Barracks, now with an unusually long cigar, arrived. Yes, yes, we would meet at the usual place, usual table. The news was good. Yes, he did know about Dweiri but he would be dealt with later. Must be careful, there was a chance the Cubans were using Nasser agents to monitor everything. Better not rely on Ali; after all he was pro-Nasser. No, No. . . . There was no reason to see Cuvellier, enough to give her his love. He agreed with giving Dreize half of the money now – why not! The rest later.

The trial lasted three days. Cuvellier, claiming to be a gainfully employed architect in Switzerland, said she had come to Beirut as a tourist, met Green on the plane and befriended him without knowing anything about his shady activities. Our documentation supported Cuvellier's claim of architectural employment in Switzerland and everything spoke of Cuvellier wanting to go home.

Judge Dreize hammered Green with loaded questions while the latter screamed innocence. All the pieces fell into place with the precision of a Lebanese plot.

The verdict was what we wanted. Cuvellier: innocent; Green: fifteen years in jail. That evening Cuvellier and I celebrated until dawn. Whatever reserve she had left disappeared; she was a little girl full of games and giggles openly holding my hand and obviously very, very happy. Both the Lebanese and Western press accepted the decision and Ali

Bitar, as he placed a drink in front of me, said, 'I am happy for you but stay away from these things in the future.'

Years after, the full story of Cuvellier-Green as part of a much bigger plot became known. They were the team sent to Beirut while other teams of twos had been dispatched to other international money centres to do the same thing: exchange Cuban pesos in anticipation of their discontinuation so that Cuban currency would be undermined internationally to the extent of not being accepted ever again.

The money was bought from Batista by the CIA at a considerable discount after he was told of its impending discontinuation. Cuvellier was an operative, Green was a smuggler recruited to help with this job only. He jeopardized everything when, after exchanging the first two hundred thousand dollars, he, among other things, spent $5,000 on a local whore. Rather than go on, Cuvellier scuttled the whole operation by casting doubt on the source of the currency bills to a local money-changer. She thought, the greater the amount exchanged, the greater would be the penalty when caught as a result of Green's behaviour.

Whatever I know about Paul Klee, Federico Garcia Lorca and the Mozart piano pieces, to mention only a few things, I owe to Cuvellier. Though our entangled personal relationship continued for years, she never told me what happened to the rest of the money. She lives in Spain now. John Green died after leaving prison and James Russell Barracks died mysteriously in Nigeria.

'There weren't many women there: it was a man's place. As a woman you'd have to have a good reason to be there.'

Lorice Parker, vice president, Mellon Bank

'Ali Bitar was an amazing barman, a gentleman barman. Sure he was trained in London but that isn't the point; it is the respect people had for him which made him special.'

Jean Bertolet, former manager, St George Hotel

'Don't forget how the staff behaved towards people they didn't want to see again, particularly women out for excitement. It was the most delicate way of handling things — making them feel unwelcome.'

Harry Kondakjian, AP photo editor

16

SISTERS OF MEN

The number of notable ladies who used the bar enough to have left an impression is few indeed and they divide along clearly identifiable lines. Half went there because of their husbands; they came to the bar as part of a team or alone to support their husbands' work. The second group were the loners; they managed to penetrate the clubby masculine atmosphere because of what they did or because their personal attributes overcame the obvious obstacles which pointed towards their exclusion.

To underscore the masculine character of the bar and its inherent rejection of things feminine, I should like to retell a story which involved my friend John Bulloch, now Middle East editor of *The Independent* and formerly Middle East correspondent of the *Daily Telegraph*.

In the early seventies the owner of the *Daily Telegraph*, Lord Hartwell, suggested to his editors that they should send special writers to Beirut to produce appropriate features on the economically booming city which incorporated the best in East and West. One of these writers was Dame Rebecca West who arrived in Beirut with a lady companion in tow and installed herself at the St George Hotel. Bulloch, then the *Telegraph* man in Beirut, duly met Rebecca West and companion and squired them around. On the first evening Bulloch met the ladies for a drink at the bar and, by way of making conversation, identified various colourful people there. West took it all in her stride. Her companion did not.

Two days later Bulloch received an imperious call from Rebecca West 'to come here immediately'. Bulloch got to the bar in a hurry to find Rebecca West waiting, nursing a very large scotch. West's companion, a less travelled and less worldly lady, had taken Bulloch's description of the bar characters literally and, in West's words: 'She sees spies everywhere; she thinks she might be assassinated. Please send her home.' Though the situation wasn't that serious, John Bulloch arranged the gullible companion's departure from Beirut on the first flight out to London.

Generally speaking, the machinations which took place at the bar belonged to a world inhabited by men. Women either found out that they couldn't relate to the place and felt uncomfortable there or, much like West's companion, they viewed it with fear. I know of several wives of news correspondents and businessmen who never set foot inside the place during lengthy stays in Beirut and others who thought one visit was enough.

Yet some ladies did go there, both with partners and alone, and, as we will see, unattached ones made their mark on the bar's story. Those who went there for the occasional social drink are not our concern, even when they behaved as if they belonged to the place. Our focus of attention is the ladies who used the bar as an extension of what their husbands did, when the husband's activity was important; and others whose rôle in the bar was a singular happening unto itself, not to mention their successful invasion of the men's redoubt.

The first lady to use the bar freely, without being relegated to the ranks of a silent observer, was Kate Tweedie Roosevelt, the wife of Archie Roosevelt, the first and perhaps most effective CIA station chief in Beirut. This was in the early fifties, when the identity of top CIA operatives was more of an open secret than it is now and Kate's visits to the bar, alone or with Archie, were worthy of the wife of a super-spy.

Aristocratic, attractive, multilingual, Kate was her own person as well as Archie's wife. Not only did she drive around Beirut with the panache of a local taxi driver, she paid little attention to other aspects of diplomatic proto-col and she would engage people from garbage collectors to presidential hopefuls in passionate conversation about conditions in Lebanon and the Middle East. To locals who didn't know Kate by her first name or couldn't wrap their tongue around the long last name and others whose position did not allow for familiarity, she was Mrs Spy (*Mart al Jassous*).

When in the bar with her husband, Kate Roosevelt was a full participant in whatever he did, and certainly spoke her own mind even when disagreeing with Archie. Alone, she was what the Arabs call 'a sister of men' (*Ikut El Rjal*) and this meant holding her own be it in political discussion or the consumption of drink. The rules governing the behaviour of spies' wives, if they existed, were subordinated to Kate's individualism and she was once heard scolding a British diplomat about his country's 'stupid, outdated behaviour'.

Though undoubtedly acquainted with the workings of the complex world around her, including the secrets of America's intelligence efforts, Kate was very much a female. Her frequent bar visits provided a much needed softening agent, her femininity, good looks and elegance were a welcome addition to the dryness of atmosphere which go with the exclusivity of men's gathering places, and the bar regulars welcomed her presence openly. The fact that Kate was extremely intelligent and up-to-date with current affairs challenged the basis of men's complaints about the presence of women. I mentioned Kate's name to nine of the old bar regulars who had known her and all agreed that she flung the door wide open for other women to use the place.

If Kate Roosevelt was the pioneer diplomat's wife, then Nina Alpherew, wife of the Middle East's Pepsi Cola general manager Ted Alpherew, paved the way for the entry into the bar of the businessman's wife with equal gusto. Nina and Ted lived at the St George Hotel for six years, from 1952 to 1958, and because of Ted's frequent travel throughout the region, she learned to use the bar alone and, in the process, overcame men's prejudice against business wives, becoming a most regular among regulars who unfailingly bought her own round of drinks.

Even by Beirut standards, the Alpherews were an exotic,

worldly couple. Ted was Russian by background and Nina was Armenian-Iranian but both were naturalized American citizens who between them spoke thirteen languages. Elegant in appearance and behaviour, they looked like transplants from the 1920s Paris Ritz crowd, always dressed as if they were attending the social event of the decade. Nina saw her role as supporting Ted, a glamorous corporate wife, and in the case of the bar the requirements were stringent.

Coca Cola, Pepsi's international rival, was banned from the Arab countries, blacklisted because its management, particularly its chairman and New York politician Jimmy Byrn, supported Israel and raised money for Zionist causes. This gave Pepsi a free hand in one of the world's most lucrative soft drink markets and it was up to Ted and Nina Alpherew to capitalize on this monopolistic situation and guard against any changes in Arab attitude which might endanger it.

When it came to Nina's supportive function this meant that the usual feminine barbs against a husband's corporate competitors had a political tilt to them, so, instead of claiming taste superiority for Pepsi, Nina got into the business of accusing Coca Cola of political crimes against the Arabs. To do this effectively Nina kept herself informed as to the amounts of money donated by Byrn to Israel and recited these figures to any willing listener. She carried the activity to its sinister natural conclusion by comparing such nefarious activity with the neglect shown towards Palestinian refugees.

Most of the seasoned bar regulars took Nina's offerings with a pinch of salt but many visitors sat open-mouthed while Nina recited Coke's list of crimes. Some who were new to things Middle Eastern and to the bar would genuinely urge Nina to become a spokesman for Arab causes at the United Nations.

One could make much of what Nina said and did, seriously and otherwise, but there is no denying her talent: she had an uncanny ability to adapt herself to the specific atmosphere of the bar and the Middle East. She was in the business of promoting Ted Alpherew's career and would stop at nothing to do it.

The third example of a wife bar frequenter was Shirley Mecklin, wife of *Time*'s John Mecklin. Shirley simply refused to be a bar widow and came to the place with and without her husband. But as the bar press represented the largest group of users of the bar and because other correspondents found Shirley's behaviour might prove contagious, most of the press behaved in a hostile, ungallant way towards her, in spite of her charm, good looks and superior intellect. They totally opposed her presence.

Unlike Kate Roosevelt and Nina Alpherew, Shirley didn't go to the bar to support husband John; she went there because she thoroughly and vocally objected to women's exclusion from the place. She saw in the men's attitude a sexist insult which she refused to swallow.

The difference between her and the Roosevelts and Alpherews went further; Mecklin was not supportive of his wife's forays into the bar, nor for that matter did she get support from other correspondents' wives. Still she persisted, with sad results: this and John's long absences in various parts of the Middle East exacerbated an already shaky marriage which produced a separation and eventual divorce.

Shirley Mecklin's failure should not detract from the nobility of her effort. The liberal-minded, University of Chicago-educated advocate of women's rights would have been amazed at the success enjoyed by the woman who followed her in the annals of the place. Afifa Iskander should have had more problems because she was self-educated, Iraqi and a professional singer. In Iraq, being a singer was tantamount to being a whore, yet even in Beirut, at the bar, Iskander's problem was not finding acceptance by men but keeping her entourage of male admirers to a manageable size.

In many ways Afifa Iskander was the strangest female bar frequenter of all time. She had come to Beirut from Baghdad at the end of 1958 and lived at the hotel. In Baghdad she had been Iraq's leading female vocalist and had owned the city's top cabaret, the Mecca for the country's high and mighty, many of whom had befriended the owner. When the government of Iraq was overthrown in July 1958, many of her friends had lost favour and she herself was sufficiently identified with the old government to fear for her own safety. Eventually she managed to flee to the shelter of Beirut, the hotel and the bar.

The Iskander who arrived in Beirut was forty, a member of Iraq's Christian minority and Arab, plump with a pretty, round face and a fresh smile. Surprisingly, she spoke English and French, read a lot and was completely at ease in the company of Arab men, who treated her as an equal. Rumour had it that she had been the model for the heroine in Desmond Stewart's novel *A Woman Besieged*, a story of a power hungry courtesan who manipulated the fortunes of a country from the chamber room.

No less important than Iskander's past was her awesome presence in the bar as a national symbol for Iraqi exiles operating out of Beirut. She occupied a table in the corner of the bar on a daily basis and one might say it was the closest anyone came to holding court in the place. Former ministers, generals, businessmen, political hopefuls and others came to pay their respects to her regularly. She talked politics, the good old days, books, and mercilessly teased her visitors about their sexual proclivities and extra-marital affairs while punctuating all this with extremely funny imitations of Americans abroad and Englishmen discussing a country garden. She towered above the men who came to visit her and they treated her with a respect bordering on reverence.

But Afifa Iskander's unique position was not recognized only by exiles. The new Iraqi government, the one that drove her out of Baghdad, viewed her with equal respect. In 1959 the Iraqi ambassador to Lebanon arrived at Afifa's bar court unannounced and invited himself to join her, much to the consternation of others there who espoused different political ideologies. The others left after a polite interlude and the ambassador apologized, telling her that fear of not being received was behind the manner of his visit.

The ambassador then pleaded with Iskander to return home to Iraq and not to join the opposition in exile. He promised her safe passage back to Iraq, the return of her club and a long-term singing contract with Iraqi Broadcasting. Iskander listened carefully but sent the ambassador away without an answer; she asked for time to consider his offer.

By then the bar press and spies had noticed this woman's exalted position among her countrymen and had decided she was an excellent source of information, the depository of all the secrets of what was happening in her country. As the struggle for the control of Iraq by pro- and anti-communist forces was one of the leading stories of the time, everyone interested in the fate of Iraq tried to befriend Iskander.

During her two-year stay at the hotel and visits to the bar Iskander turned down at least one offer to work for the CIA and did not grant a single on the record interview though she obviously enjoyed the company of journalists, describing their work as a 'fun job'.

She eventually returned to Iraq after the government of the country agreed to her conditions: no songs in praise of the régime, a refusal to submit to interrogation about her old connections and the return of all her old property. Now she has retired with a generous pension from the Iraqi government and her house along the Tigris River is a larger version of her bar court, an old-fashioned salon for dozens of people who seek wisdom from an old lady who attained a most unusual position in a country that does not accord women or singers much respect. Iraqi governments have come and gone, but Iraq has only one Afifa Iskander.

Enough has been said about Myrna Bustani as part owner of the St George and the only female member ever of Lebanon's parliament but she deserves more as someone who during the sixties and seventies frequented the bar and grill room. Myrna's worldly achievements are matched by what the Lebanese call 'lightness of heart', a most attractive presence, which glittered during her visits to the bar and grill room.

Most of the time Myrna's presence in the bar was an extension of her parliamentary role and due to the fact that her commitment to elegance and good food could only be satisfied there. Very often she came to the bar as a prelude to lunching at the grill room in the company of octogenarian former Prime Minister Hussein Oweini. They had loved each other's company: she adored his gracious old ways and he revelled in her charming presence.

Still there was more to the meetings of these two than met the eye. The political inclinations and voting record of the only female member of parliament carried considerable weight; she spoke for more than her constituency, she spoke for fifty per cent of the population. As such, she had considerable political clout, her vote on issues was watched closely by the country's contenders for power, many of whom followed her lead in an attempt to capitalize on the rising tide of feminism.

Oweini was as sensitive to her power as her charm and was among the many who courted her; there is no doubt as to her visible joy in his attentions. But she always maintained her independence, took special care to protect the power inherent in her position. In the words of an admiring former colleague: 'Anyone who took Myrna for granted had a surprise coming.' If she viewed her joint ownership of the St George Hotel as a national trust, then she treated her position in parliament with the same protective jealousy.

In the bar Myrna engaged the journalists, spies and businessmen in open debate on regional and local issues, always probing and trying to learn. She would solicit the opinion of a writer, doorman or bartender, carefully observing their fear in dealing with their bosses' boss. She was known to turn to a journalist seeking her opinion on a thorny subject and twist the question around: 'What do you think?' or 'You have not said anything yet, you tell me.'

Myrna Bustani's dedication to learning evolved into a commitment to what mattered, a distaste for Lebanese infighting coupled with a desire to transplant the spirit of devotion which enveloped hotel workers to Lebanon as a whole. Not only did she contribute to charities and open schools and clinics, she addressed herself to sound municipal planning and beautification.

The bar was always a different place when Myrna Bustani

was in it; it was more fun and interesting and one truly felt the presence of someone who was incorporating the best of what the place had to offer into a positive act. When I told Ali Bitar of Myrna's view of the St George as a national treasure, he paused and then said 'She's one herself.'

Besides Iskander and Bustani, the third Arab lady to carve herself a niche in the legend of the bar was Mai Jumblatt, the widow of Lebanese leader Kamal Jumblatt and mother of Druze community leader Walid, the jean-attired war lord of one of Lebanon's religious groups.

Mai Jumblatt frequented the bar during the fifties, sixties and seventies because her husband was an austere, yoga-practising socialist who frowned on the place and what happened there. Mai, who lived apart from her husband most of the time, considered her visits to the bar part of her rebellion against women's position in Lebanese society.

Elegant, Swiss-educated Mai spoke Arabic and English with a charming French accent, recited poetry in all three languages and had the figure and elegance of a Dior model. Not only was she outspoken about the right of women to be in a man's stronghold, she lived up to her complaints and appeared there in the company of female friends.

To begin with, the bar press viewed Mai's presence with considerable unease, though they liked and admired her. They simply feared the consequences of talking to her and befriending her, feared what her husband might do to them. In time she overcame this hurdle and became an unofficial spokeswoman for anything to do with the status of Arab women – and more. She earned a position as a reliable sounding-board on many issues which mattered.

While she had no interest in personal glory, there is little doubt that her frequent visits with the bar press contributed towards a better image of Arab women and the benefits which would result from their total emancipation. She held herself as an example of what might be: in the words of my admiring father, 'an overwhelming piece of evidence'.

If Jumblatt, Bustani and Iskander represented a new breed of Arab women and Mecklin, Alpherew and Roosevelt the

Western woman determined to assume her rightful position, then American diplomat Mary Hawthorne was the real McCoy; she competed with men of the bar in their own fields, on their own turf.

A political officer at the US Embassy in Beirut during 1960–63, Hawthorne became a bar regular with the full knowledge and approval of her ambassador and in all likelihood of the State Department in Washington. Because recognized embassy officers had spent little time at the bar, people assumed that Mary's assignment had to do with her femininity and Nordic good looks and their appeal to local journalists and politicians. Initially this thought was strengthened by the Arabs welcoming her and others resenting her presence.

Objections to her presence notwithstanding, Hawthorne moved forward undaunted; her only concern was the advancement of American interests and her career. She became a roving diplomat who used the bar as a headquarters where she met local politicians and journalists and went further by enticing usually reticent exiles into opening up and telling her what they knew.

Lebanese presidential hopeful Raymond Edde kept her company and debated issues with her; Iraqi exile Jameel Abdel Wahab would hold on to information emanating from his country until 'Miss Mary' was there and brooding PLO types found it easy to share their dreams with her. The Egyptian Embassy, then openly anti-American, became wary of Mary's activities and discussed plans to discredit her, a testimony to her effectiveness. Because her everyday behaviour was above reproach, the Egyptians failed.

Using a pretty woman as bait might be considered a snide American attempt to master an old ploy but there is no doubt about her hard work and effectiveness. If Mary Hawthorne was a twist on an old game, a latter day Mata Hari without dirt, then so be it. She succeeded where other diplomats and spies failed.

The seven women discussed, along with Eleanor Philby and, briefly, Nicole Cuvellier, represented the ladies of the bar, ones who left an imprint on its rich history. While no two of them were alike in looks or behaviour, they had a major attribute in common: they were ahead of their time, pioneers who combined femininity with a desire to be counted and they all succeeded – even Shirley Mecklin.

These women had to do everything exceptionally well. Bustani's position may have been unique but she gave it meaning through her personal commitment and achievements. Jumblatt's championship of women's rights could easily be applied to women's plight everywhere in the world and Iskander broke down all obstacles and became a national institution in a country which considers women second-class citizens. Mecklin rejected her secondary role, while Alpherew subordinated local conditions to her goal, and Roosevelt and Hawthorne discarded the politeness of diplomatic etiquette and performed admirably, conquering the doubts of all ill-wishers. They were a very remarkable collection of women. Honour to them, honour to these sisters of men.

17

A WORLD NO MORE

Ali Bitar, the legendary barman of the St George Hotel, lives in Santa Monica, California, with his wife and two youngest daughters. His apartment is modestly but tastefully furnished, a far cry from his palatial six-bedroom house in Khalde, along the seashore on the southern outskirts of Beirut. His two sons and eldest daughter have married and moved away but remain in constant, reverent contact with their parents.

Ali is seventy but doesn't look it; he looks more like a man in his fifties. He attributes his unwrinkled looks and trim figure to all the years he spent on his feet at the bar and his continued devotion to daily exercise which now includes long walks along the Santa Monica ocean front. Ali loves California and is sensitive to its beauty and what it has to offer – the sea, mountains and fresh produce – but he laments being 'far away from things; by the time we hear about a happening in the Lebanon it is all over'. During his daily walks along the ocean front Ali remembers the good old Beirut days and the forty years of constant excitement he spent at the bar.

Now Ali is ready to talk, to unburden himself of the thoughts and memories which visit him regularly. Behind his decision to talk is loneliness; the normal old-age condition is exacerbated by the distance which separates him from Beirut and the Middle East and the absence of people with whom he could discuss such things. This and the conviction that 'his bar' isn't about to be resurrected translate into a desire to set the record straight, 'to tell it the way it really was': To Ali, setting the record straight means correcting some impressions and defending some people but it in no

188

way should mean 'scandalizing people; I am too old for that'.

The bar was Ali's life; slightly amended, its history becomes Ali's life story because he grew up there and participated, directly and indirectly, in the creation of its atmosphere, the source of its mystique. As a young waiter he had learned to copy people's manner of dress and behaviour; then eventually, through osmosis, he became educated in the worlds of espionage, foreign reporting and international business. Though his appreciation of the world which whirled around him occasionally betrays his lack of formal education, he is nevertheless an excellent judge of the participants in these trades. For example, when Ali compares the correspondents of popular and serious newspapers his keenness of observation is most revealing; it carries with it a freshness which produces a clear, crisp picture of what the differences between them are, which, if carried to its conclusion, can easily lead to discarding old theories and adopting new ones.

Born at a small village near Latakia in north-west Syria in a pious Moslem household, Ali and his parents moved to Beirut in 1934, when Syria and Lebanon were under French rule and the smaller country offered better opportunities. After a couple of short-lived jobs, he was hired from among a hundred and fifty applicants to wait at tables at the bar. Ali teasingly plays games regarding his employment, insisting on feigning ignorance about his selection. He was undoubtedly raw and uneducated in matters of dress and behaviour, but the still present twinkle in the eyes, the pleasant smile and natural politeness provide a ready answer. Still, his awareness of his shortcomings appears to have propelled him forward, made him learn through exposure and by going to school whenever time permitted; eventually this desire 'to know' created the worldly, sophisticated man admired by hundreds if not thousands of customers on whose lives he left a tremendous impression.

I began my interview of Ali by asking about his attitude towards the various national groups which frequented the bar and was presented with an unexpected answer: his least favourite people in the whole world were the Scots and the Saudis. The surprising entry, the Scots, used the bar during the Second World War when they came to Beirut with the Allied forces which freed Lebanon from Vichy France.

Ali remembers the Scots: 'They drank a lot, sang a lot, exposed themselves [wore kilts] and usually left the bar without paying.' The Scots' ways had contrasted sharply with what Ali had always known – the sophisticated, polite ways of French colonialists who, until pushed out by the Brits, had been the bar's mainstay.

Even a World War didn't stop Ali and the then bar manager from taking exception to the new arrivals and naively posting signs declaring the bar out of limits for Scottish officers. Twenty-four hours after the signposting act of bravado Ali and his colleague were in a British army jail accused by a Scots major of trading in contraband cigarettes. Lengthy negotiations led to a truce: Ali and his boss were released after a promise to take down the sign in return for a commitment by the Scots 'not to sing or cross their legs'. According to Ali, they still didn't pay their bills and he still doesn't like them.

The Saudis came later, in the late fifties, after their country began realizing substantial income from oil. They came to Beirut to summer or do business or both and, like people with money everywhere, they saw fit to frequent the best places. Ali's memories of the Saudis are damning. He speaks of the Saudis being 'the biggest national problem we ever had at the bar. They stayed the miserable way they were; they never improved. This is true of Saudis from the royal family all the way down . . . but if members of one's royal family don't know how to behave then what does one expect from the rest. They all were ill-mannered.'

There were a lot of ugly bar incidents involving Saudis which Ali remembers with sadness and barely controlled anger. A Saudi sheikh drank himself into such a state he began drinking cognac out of the Remi Martin bottle and arrogantly refused to use a glass, which was followed by an invitation to leave. The commander of Saudi Arabia's land forces, a general and close friend of His Majesty King Saud, offered a Lebanese businessman sitting next to him in the bar 50,000 Lebanese lira (sixteen thousand dollars) for one night of pleasure with the businessman's wife, who herself had to suffer the indignity of listening to the indecent offer. A member of the Saudi royal family staying at the hotel locked the temporary secretary sent to help him in the bathroom of his suite after she refused his advances, kept her there and descended to the bar to hold court. To Ali the Saudis were unlike the Kuwaitis and other Gulf Arabs who had been exposed to the world as traders; the Saudis 'got the money too suddenly and didn't know how to behave'.

Other national groups solicit nothing but kind words: 'gentlemanly' for the English, 'folksy and friendly' for the Americans; the Russians are 'full of life', the French 'so-phisticated' and the Jordanians and Egyptians 'exceptionally polite'. These sweeping descriptions of national character are very important to Ali because they are the attributes which he used to assess members of the professions who came to the bar and whom he knew best: journalists, spies and businessmen.

Using the mention of spies as an opening, I asked Ali to tell me more about them and their use of the bar as a gathering place and listening post for their work. Suddenly, as if it were second nature to him, Ali took on several different attitudes at the same time. He became light and amusing, reflective and reverent, slightly cynical, occasionally dismissive, and finally reverted to his barman's training and became silent, but not until formulating a challenge: 'It is impossible to tell the number of spies who came to the bar. There were more of them than you or anyone else ever knew.' When my lack of reaction left him uncertain he went forward: 'Yes, the place was full of spies; perhaps there were more spies than journalists. After all, most of the journalists were also spies.'

My more specific questions about spies and spying received three types of answers. There were direct answers about rec-ognized people such as Philby; Ali described him as having been a master spy . . . 'to drink as much as he did without saying anything, remarkable'. Indirect answers were meant to lead me to investigate other situations . . . 'Mr Fistere was important . . . check on him, on his relationship with Philby.'

And last was the evasive, empty reply, the equivalent of a refusal to answer . . . 'Mr Barracks befriended everyone – that's all I know.'

Ali's personal involvement in espionage work is now admitted. His own account is that he worked for Lebanese Security from the early fifties; he was recruited by Farid Chehab, the legendary head of Internal Security and Intelligence. He claims that he was never paid for his work because he operated in accordance with an odd brief which afforded him considerable discretionary powers 'to report those who endangered the security of Lebanon'. This broad outline of his intelligence duties resulted in a number of reports which led to the deportation from Beirut of a number of minor operatives including one American, G.M. To Ali, polite, discreet, security-conscious spies were not a problem, but loud, indiscreet ones presented him with a problem which he shared with Lebanese Security to the bar's and Lebanon's mutual advantage.

The connection between Ali and Lebanese Intelligence led to a question about working for the British indirectly because, according to MI6 agent Anthony Cavendish, the bar was used as a meeting place between former MI6 head Maurice Oldfield and Chehab, Ali's recruiter and contact. Ali reflected briefly, admitted he didn't know anything about that and closed by labelling his work as having been all 'for Lebanon'.

There was an inevitable return to the subject of the most famous bar spy of them all, Kim Philby. Ali weighed his words carefully . . . 'We [the staff] knew little of his background and the complex stuff . . . still, there was something strange going on. He and his wife didn't seem to have any friends; people didn't behave naturally in their presence . . .' My question about an American CIA monitoring operation received a full and satisfactory answer in the form of a

question, 'How do you monitor someone who never said anything even when he drank enough for a dozen people . . . ?'
Noting my disappointment at the fact that there was nothing
new in his answers about Philby, Ali took the initiative:
'I believe Fistere was as big as Philby . . . he controlled a
whole country [Jordan] and he was involved in Mr Philby's
situation . . . he was so friendly towards Kim – phew. There
was another big one but I am not ready to talk about that.
. . . No, I won't.'

This was my chance to ask Ali about a former head of the
International Red Cross, one D.D.T., a Swiss national and
one-time bar regular. Ali leaned back and stared at me as if
to say 'you've done your homework', then, breathing audibly,
said, 'I remember that he went to Israel all the time, directly
from Beirut because he had diplomatic immunity.' Then he
stopped and sighed: 'Why don't you ask the Americans about
him? They were after him; ask them.'

Though he admitted that the CIA, MI6 and the KGB all
offered him jobs which he turned down, Ali refused to reveal
the individual names of those who tried to recruit him. This
was followed by a refusal to answer questions about the
Hotel Workers' Union, a labour union of which he was an
officer and which was suspected of fronting for Russia and
the KGB.

My last question about spies and spying concerned an
English journalist suspected of working for MI6. Hinting
heavily that the man in question was a freelance, part-time
spy who did occasional work for the British, Ali left things
at that and moved on to discuss the mercenary spies, those
who sold their wares to the highest bidder. With undisguised
condescension Ali admitted that 'nobody wanted to deal
with the whores of the businessmen. . . . There was no
way to determine how many times they sold the same piece
of information. . . . The bar was too good for that nonsense.
The bar spies were true professionals.'

The bar press were our next topic of discussion and the
mere mention of them produced a big smile and a description
of them as having been a barman's dream clientele: 'Drinkers,

spenders and mostly very polite . . . also they were interested in what we [the bar staff] had to say. . . . They made us feel important.' Remembering his previous comments, Ali concluded, 'The ones who doubled as spies were the ones who shied from talking to the staff. . . . They felt awkward about engaging us in conversation, in asking us any questions. . . . This was one way to tell . . .'

The corner of Ali's mind which stores his attitudes towards the various national groups which frequented the bar applied itself to journalists with amusing results: 'The Americans gave the impression of working harder but the British knew what they were doing; they were much more deliberate. They didn't like each other; the British made fun of the Americans all the time, more than the Americans did of them. We had few French journalists, they usually were good, very good. The funniest lot were the Australians – strange, a bit British, a bit American, loud but very likeable.'

Pursuing more specific examples of the use of the bar by journalists, I asked Ali about news stories which originated there. This provoked long, happy laughter which wasn't justified by the question . . . 'I myself started one which led to a major crisis, an international crisis. . . . I also withheld information which would have made big news . . . with big repercussions.'

Ali continued, 'In the fifties . . . it was really big . . . in the fifties there happened to be two customers in the bar who were obviously outsiders, new to the place. . . . American army officers stationed in Turkey who were in charge of training the Turkish army. . . . They had too much to drink and talked. . . . Mr Bell [James Bell of *Time* magazine] was in the bar and I told him that they were telling funny stories, jokes, about how untrainable the Turkish army was . . . well, Mr Bell moved closer to them and listened . . . they talked about new tanks and planes which America had given to Turkey. . . . Well, Mr Bell wrote a story in *Time* which caused trouble between the US and Turkey. He reported what they said and added that the information must have reached Russia because the bar was full of Russian spies

194

some of whom were waiters. . . . God knows what resulted from this but it was big. . . .

'When Mr Kim [Philby] disappeared we [the bar staff] had a lot of fun . . . journalists from all over the world came wanting to know the smallest piece of information about him . . . so we told them jokes, we invented them. . . . Abu Khalil [the Armenian bartender] told someone that Mr Kim ate a lot of onions, loads and loads. . . . I think the guy wrote a story about it . . . we traded in what Mr Kim drank, whisky, told another group that he drank gin, then we moved to vodka, which intrigued some journalists because they wanted to find out whether it was Russian vodka. During this period, right after Mr Kim defected, the regular bar spies disappeared. . . . Mr Ashworth [a British businessman unknown to the writer], Mr Richards [*Financial Times*], Mr Eveland and Mr Fistere. . . . I guess that they didn't want to see all the amatuers who came in to discuss Mr Kim.

'Yes, there was another time besides Mr Bell's story when my own behaviour affected things in the Middle East, in this case the future of a country . . . Syria. I knew that a coup was about to take place in Syria but I decided not to tell anyone . . .' The long story, which I have verified with others, originated with one of the top tribal sheikhs in the Middle East, Fawaz Al Shalan, Emir of the Rwalahs. Shalan, who had a younger brother named Lawrence after the legendary Lawrence of Arabia, was a bar regular who drank more than most. His tribe was scattered throughout the Arabian Peninsula but he was its sheikh of sheikhs and his power was undisputed. Some of his followers were officers in the Syrian army and it was they who put tribal loyalty ahead of one to country and told him of an impending coup d'état against Syria's dictator Adib Shaishakly.

Thinking that Ali would give or sell the news to a member of the bar press, Shalan informed Ali of the plot, including the names of the officers and army units involved. Disclosure, hoped Shalan, would nip the plot in the bud and what better way than to use Ali and remain above the fray. But Ali did not like Shaishakly and was happy to sit on the news and allow the coup to take place. Shaishakly was overthrown with serious implications for Syria and the rest of the Middle East. The obvious question as to whether Ali acted alone or after consulting someone else is one he refuses to answer.

Asking Ali to identify the most memorable moment of his career came naturally, the way it would have had I been interviewing a retired politician or general. He showed no hesitation; instead he spoke like a man who had had given a great deal of time to reviewing his life in detail and had already isolated the things in it that mattered.

'Meeting the president of Lebanon was the high point of my career . . . life . . . but I don't want his name or the time mentioned. He sent me a special messenger asking to see me but requested that I tell no one, not even my boss. Of course I went to the palace the following day . . .

'We were by ourselves having Turkish coffee and the President asked for my help. Prince —————— of Saudi Arabia was in exile in Lebanon; he was opposed to his brother the king and spent a lot of time with the bar press attacking the policies of his country and his brother. This caused a crisis between Lebanon and Saudi Arabia because some of what Prince —————— said was reported and his brother wanted him silenced. The president wanted the prince to cease his attacks without undermining Lebanon's free atmosphere, without having to deport him or officially demand his silence. Instead he asked for my help in "handling" the prince . . .'

Ali found a way of frightening His Highness into silence by telling him that some of the newsmen in the bar were spying for his brother the king and others for Lebanese Security. That put the fear of Allah into the prince and led him to avoid the bar. A Lebanese-Saudi diplomatic crisis was averted and a special presidential messenger came to the bar to thank Ali for his successful stunt.

On another occasion, Ali, discreetly and on his own initiative, managed to undo a planned assassination of a Lebanese politician, something which could have led to a major civil disturbance if not an all-out civil war. The politician belonged to the Maronite sect from which presidents have to come and he himself had presidential ambitions. He had used the hotel as a hideaway for his secret meetings with a Moslem Lebanese woman. Not only was this type of liaison forbidden under all circumstances, but the girl came from an important political Moslem family who, according to Ali's information, were making plans to eliminate the Christian problem, to kill the lover.

Afraid of the cycle of violence which would follow such an act, Ali quickly took it upon himself to speak to both lovers. He pleaded with them to put Lebanon's national interest ahead of personal desire and bring the affair to an end. Luckily his advice was heeded and the bar press was spared the agony of explaining another Lebanese altercation to the world.

Ali is rightly proud of his achievements in life. He places the education of his children above all else and points to their successful careers with visible satisfaction. This special glow is extinguished when he talks about the change from being courted by famous politicians, spies and journalists to the humdrum middle-class life he leads in California. He finds it difficult to talk about the new models of cars and the latest episode of *Dallas* or *Dynasty*. Conversely, his neighbours find his Beirut stories about the bar, the six-bedroom house, the driver and the two maids hard to understand. Sighs Ali: 'Here a barman is just anybody. . . . I'd like to go back to Beirut . . . not to work, just to be there.'

I wanted to leave Ali happy with the thoughts of his achievements, among other things, that he once saved Lebanon from a near certain civil war, and so I made him a promise to telephone several of the bar regulars now scattered all over the world and give them his salaams. Everybody was pleased to hear Ali's news and without exception used the same word to describe the little Syrian boy who had become a pleasant part of their lives: gentleman.

A man on a Beirut rooftop leisurely pointed his rifle towards innocent people in a city street and fired at random. His nephew, curious about the purpose of the bloody exercise, asked him what he was doing. 'I am shooting people' answered the uncle.

'Why?' asked the nephew increduously.

'They pay me twenty-five pounds a head for every person I shoot.'

'How do they know how many people you've shot?'

At this point, visibly hurt at his nephew's rudeness, the man threw down the rifle and protested: 'Am I not an "honourable man"?'

Wilton Wynn, *Time* correspondent

18

LEBANON FINALE – THE BEGINNING OF TERROR

Beirut was never as vital as it was in 1973. Its rôle as a bridge between East and West had been enhanced to such an extent that it became one of the best-known, most talked about cosmopolitan centres in the world.

But while Beirut was a universe unto itself and the St George Hotel and its now famous bar exemplified the distillation of the elegance that had become the city's synonym, Lebanon's political house of cards was collapsing and, with the help of the outside world, the destruction of Lebanon, Beirut and the hotel was in the making. It is impossible to write about the end of the bar without discussing the end of Lebanon as a civilized country, and it is almost impossible to undertake the awesome task of explaining the Lebanese mess without digressing and dealing with facts that are outside the original purpose of this book and which introduce an ugly reality in the deliciously naughty reality that was the bar.

I never thought of Lebanon as a country; I always thought of the place as an idea, essentially a good idea. But by 1973 what began as a lovely idea had become obsolete, and this descent into a loss of touch with the times resulted in a savage conflict between those who wanted to maintain the old Lebanon and others equally insistent on a generic transformation.

Lebanon was created by the French. After the First World War, France inherited Syria from the reduced Ottoman Empire, and Lebanon was no more than a state within Syria. By the time the French left in 1946 they had opted to create a new independent Lebanon out of Syria because, rightly, they had decided that the territory possessed a distinct historical identity, in particular its largely Christian population.

The Lebanon to which the French granted independence in 1946, though meant to be a haven for Christians, comprised Catholics (Maronites), Greek Orthodox, Sunni Moslems, Shia Moslems, Druze and a number of smaller sects. The constitution and subsidiary documents developed to reconcile these religions in one happy country divided the high offices in the land according to religious affiliation, i.e., a Catholic president, Sunni prime minister, Shia speaker of parliament, Druze minister of defence and so on down the line, supposedly a reflection of a sect's share of the population.

The built-in weakness of the system is apparent; the slightest change in this delicate balance would demand a rearrangement of the whole structure of the country. The three elements that combined to destroy the French-engineered house of cards had gnawed at the foundations of the state for some time: a disproportionate level of population growth among the various sects, e.g., the Shias grow at a rate four times that of the Catholics; the arrival of 600,000 mostly Moslem Palestinians after the 1948 Arab-Israeli War; and the Moslems' growing affinity with the rest of the Arabs while the Christians looked towards the West for inspiration.

The internal machinery of the country failed to produce a solution to any of these problems, which got worse with time, so that by the early seventies the Shia claimed the presidency through sheer numbers; Moslems in general wanted a stronger stand against Israel; Catholics wanted the balance-disturbing Palestinians out of the country; while the Druze latched on to whichever side promised them a greater voice in the affairs of the country. On the outside, the Israelis, fearful of a Moslem-Palestinian predominance, supported the Catholics; Gadafi jumped in uninvited and financed the Sunni; Iran decided Lebanon was a Shia and not a Moslem problem; and the US tried to please everyone. Each group operating in Lebanon then changed sides a number of times and each change produced a chain reaction which led to further change and more incomprehensible chain reactions which are still with us to this day.

The ugly world of Lebanese politics began rearing its

unwelcome head in the charmed world of the bar in 1972 and 1973. Lebanese excellencies who wanted to throw in their lot with the winning side began frequenting the place to talk to journalists, spies and others to determine which side they might support; spokesmen for Palestinian and Lebanese armed groups came to the bar to do the opposite, to present their point of view; soldiers of fortune were there to offer their services to the highest bidder and changed sides over a drink or two. Life in the bar and Beirut was a long stretch of threatening quiet punctuated by acts of atrocity until these incidents of savagery became the order of the day and the nights-of-long-knives stretched into weeks and months so that, by 1975, a chaotic, multi-multi-factioned civil war was inevitable.

Takkieddine Es Solh, three times prime minister of Lebanon, summoned his nephew Khaldoun and brooded: 'Khaldoun, if they go for the St George and the rest of the hotels then there is no stopping the conflict. Something must be done to stop the fighting from engulfing this district; after all, the hotels symbolize what Beirut is all about.'

It was September 1975. The Lebanese Civil War, though deadly, had been a sporadic affair and there was still hope of containing it. The elder Solh's plea was self-explanatory. The elegant Phoenicia, Alcazar, Excelsior and Palm Beach hotels and particularly the St George had come to represent Beirut and all the wealth and sophistication it had possessed; destroying them would mean that there was no going back, that the warring factions had despaired of finding a peaceful solution.

To Khaldoun Es Solh this was a compelling reason to bring the war lords together; he was convinced that their view of the gravity of the situation was the same as his and his uncle's. A descendant of a Sunni Moslem family which had produced four prime ministers, he felt honour-bound to try to have the St George and its adjuncts declared a no-man's land, safe from the scourge of the roving militias which were devouring the heart of the once beautiful city.

The younger Solh succeeded in arranging a meeting at

the Holiday Inn Hotel where the representatives of the various combatants were present, at the time nine different groups. None of them took exception to Solh's appeal, which was a unifying force, and, during the meeting, they called each other by their first names and responded positively to the idea of preserving the symbols of Beirut the beautiful. An understanding was reached to meet on a regular basis to guarantee the implementation of the verbal gentlemen's agreement to stay clear of the hotel area. Khaldoun Es Solh had every reason to be happy with his achievement.

As the scale of fighting accelerated and got closer and closer to the St George, Solh redoubled his efforts and was assured by everybody that the hotel would be spared. Stray bullets now and again hit the building, leading most regular hotel and bar users to abandon the place for the safer parts of Beirut, but others continued to hope.

Inside the hotel *Washington Post* correspondent Jonathan Randall and CBS's Bill MacLaughlin had considered leaving but decided against it; the hotel provided them with a view of the scene of some of the most savage fighting and they thought they could always get away in time. They were the last two journalists living in what Randall called 'the most prestigious hostelry in the Middle East' and the pressures of work turned them into more regular bar visitors than before.

By the end of October 1975, the level of fighting in Beirut had become so ferocious that the participants in Lebanon's bloody civil war needed more than national symbols to deter them from their now legendary destructiveness. Each side was developing its own plans to occupy the strategically located hotel – it stood halfway between the Christian and Moslem sectors of Beirut, slightly inside the Moslem part.

The first group to occupy the hotel did so at noon, a move which caught everybody, including the highly experienced journalists, by surprise. The Tigers, a small Christian militia, came to the hotel in three motorboats and, using the element of surprise, occupied it without firing a shot. The ten or so Moslem gunmen who had been hired by the management to protect the hotel decided against resisting because they were not up to it and, in one of those Lebanese moves which confuse normal human minds, they began to fraternize with the invaders, even sharing their food, bedrooms and bad jokes.

However peaceful this occupation, it set a precedent and made it clear that the hotel had become part of the battle for Beirut, and employees and guests began to flee. The Tigers didn't stop anyone from leaving; the problem was that the news of their move provoked other militias to move their forces closer towards the hotel, leaving the place surrounded by different trigger-happy groups who couldn't be counted on to afford anyone safe passage.

Still, some felt a compulsion to try to pass through the lines of the surrounding forces and the first to go were the Dutch ambassador and his wife who got into their large BMW, hoisted the Dutch flag and, a mere hour after the occupation, drove slowly westward to the Hotel Riveria. The second people to leave were Lebanese politician Raymond Edde and US Ambassador C. McMurtie Godley who had been lunching together in the grill room. The ambassador used the still-connected telephone to fetch a bulletproof car, which picked them up and returned to the US Embassy and safety. The occupation must have coloured the conversation they were having; Edde was a candidate for the presidency of Lebanon.

In thirty-six hours, by 30 October, most of the hotel staff had departed, some performing last-minute acts of kindness like serving hot coffee to Randall, MacLaughlin and the six other guests who remained. But, to Randall's and MacLaughlin's shock, bartender Abu Khalil locked the wine cellar after removing all the drink from the bar and then departed. The two journalists who were trying to organize their own get-away had a drink in MacLaughlin's room from a whisky bottle he had there, and then, without saying a word, grabbed the bottle and glasses and went to the bar. They sat there alone, drinking whisky as if nothing had happened, and with the sound of machine-gun fire and thud of artillery as background, they talked about the bar and all the things that took place there.

Later, Randall, who had been scribbling notes all along, crossed the lobby, which was full of sleeping armed men and crates of ammunition, to where the telephones were, managed to reach his office in Washington and dictated an eyewitness report of the happenings of the day. He managed to get most of his story out before a Tiger militia man ordered him to stop. He did.

The following day all the guests left. Randall and Mac-Laughlin were picked up by another bulletproof embassy car after *Washington Post* publisher Ben Bradlee appealed to Secretary of State Henry Kissinger for help. The others moved out on foot carrying white flags; a short-lived Lebanese truce held long enough for them to make it to safer corners of Beirut, but some of the staff remained in the hotel determined to keep it working.

By nightfall Moslem militias in whose area the hotel was located began closing in on it from three sides; only the sea remained open to the besieged Tigers. Preparations were afoot for what, in the history of a civil war full of labels for human shame, was called the Battle of the Hotels.

The Tigers' control of the hotel lasted for four days, after which they withdrew the same way they had come, by motorboats, but only once they had arranged to use the sea route to bring in their stronger Christian allies, the Phalange. The news of replacement of the Tigers by the Phalange under the cover of darkness sent a shock wave through the ranks of the Moslems surrounding the hotel. They saw in the Phalange presence a greater threat to their territorial sovereignty because they were the larger, better equipped group, and so decided to mount an attack to occupy the hotel and eliminate the Christian presence.

Assault after assault of combined Moslem and Palestinian forces using heavier equipment every time failed to dislodge the Phalangists, who were kept resupplied by sea. But finally recognizing the untenability of their position, the Phalange withdrew the same way the Tigers had and the Moslems became the hotel's third occupiers.

When the Moslems took over the St George the remaining

staff and hired Moslem guards were found in the basement of the hotel literally praying for their lives. In one of those acts of stupidity which defy reason, the new occupiers released all the Moslems they had captured but chose to lock all Christians in the laundry pending a decision on what to do with them. They, the Christian workers, were falsely accused of having aided the original Christian occupation of the hotel.

The news of the uncertain fate of the Christian employees reached the Commodore Hotel through some of their freed Moslem colleagues. The bar press had regrouped at the Commodore and made it the news headquarters for Western Beirut. They received the news about the captured employees with shocked silence and utter helplessness – except for Abu Saïd.

Abu Saïd, a Palestinian with wide connections inside the PLO and Moslem forces, ran to the PLO headquarters and demanded a meeting with Arafat, but neither the latter nor his deputy in command was there. Finally Abu Saïd spoke to Abu Hassan Salameh, a PLO commander who was later killed by an Israeli hit squad, and pleaded with him for the safety of the St George's Christian workers in captivity. In the middle of answering tens of telephone calls and greeting unscheduled visitors, Salameh got the gist of Abu Saïd's request and, throwing his hands up in the air in a gesture of helplessness, shouted: 'I don't have the time to do anything about it. The telephone lines have been severed. If you want to save them here's a piece of paper ordering their release – take my jeep and driver.' Abu Saïd thanked Salameh and ran out.

The jeep with a driver and companion sped towards the St George Hotel with Abu Saïd in the back, his one concession to the firing which was directed at the hotel from Christian positions across the bay a steel helmet too small for him. Thirty yards from the hotel, Abu Saïd jumped out of the jeep and ran into the lobby breathlessly, waving the tiny piece of paper. The commander of the hotel occupiers began questioning Abu Saïd as to whether the order was genuine but relented when Abu Saïd volunteered to be kept there until it was verified, provided the hostages were released.

There were eighteen hostages in the laundry room. Without exception they had expected to be executed. They realized everything was all right the moment they saw their friend Abu Saïd. Crying and sobbing, some shaking so violently they were unable to walk, they were loaded into four cars carrying improvised white flags, and driven to the Commodore Hotel and safety.

A cheering press corps gave them a champagne welcome, but when one of the hostages raised his glass to toast 'the old days', Abu Saïd buried his head in his knees and began to cry.

Now the hotel is no more; it stands like an empty haunted house blackened on two sides, the one facing Moslem Beirut and the other Christian Beirut across the bay, as if both sides had willed its destruction, which they truly did. In spite of my obvious affection for the place and the good will I harbour towards Myrna Bustani and the hotel's other owners, I hope that it will be kept as it is, a monument to human folly. I can hear the voices of Philby, Fistere and Barracks, see the faces of Afifa Iskandar, Mai Jumblatt and Mary Hawthorne, and indulge in edifying conversations with Alsop, Chancellor and Delmer. Rebuilding the St George would be the criminal equivalent of remaking *Casablanca*.

INDEX

A., R., 132–3
Abdallah, Radi, 19, 53–5, 66, 67, 68, 69, 89–91
Abu Saïd (Mohamad Nimr Audeh), 149, 150–3, 207–8
Aburish, Abu Saïd, 3, 18, 19, 20, 21, 24, 27, 29, 36, 40, 42, 43, 44, 50, 54, 55, 61–4, 67, 69–70, 73, 75, 85, 118–19, 120, 121, 139
Adams, Michael, 50
Aerospatiale, 113–14
Al Ahram, 19
Al Youm, 26, 58, 158
Allumedine, Sheikh Najib, 13, 112, 116–17
Alpherew, Nina, 179–80, 187
Alpherew, Ted, 179–80
Alsop, Joe, 5, 36, 37, 38, 44–5, 69–70, 71
American Friends of the Middle East, 94
Anthology of Great Spy Stories, An, 82
Arab Air Carriers Organization, 116
Arab Boycott Office, 124
Arab Higher Committee, 150
Arab League, 88, 124, 149
Aramco, 118, 121, 122
Arida, Carlos, 112
Arslan, Emir Majid, 20, 22, 23, 26, 32
Ashworth, Mr, 195

B., A.-R., 134–5
Badr, S., 126
Barazani, Mulla Mustapha Al, 56
Barracks, James Russell, 3, 11, 22, 23, 24, 31, 32, 66, 67, 68, 69, 70, 80, 82, 86–9, 147, 163–4, 167, 168, 169–70, 171, 172, 173, 192
Bazian, Amin Hafez, 22, 23

Bedarian, Joseph, 18, 24
Bedas, Yusuf, 111, 127–8, 129
Beeston, Richard, 16, 32
Beirut, 5–8
Bell, James, 194
Bertolet, Jean, 5, 9, 13, 175
Bitar, Ali, 9, 11, 13, 17, 18, 19, 24, 26, 29, 41, 42, 61, 66, 67, 77, 79, 130, 134, 149, 170–1, 173, 175, 185, 188–97
Boeing, 125–6
Bouchow, John, 21, 22, 24, 25, 26, 27, 29, 30, 32
Bradlee, Ben, 206
Breidy, Mansour, 9, 41
Brewer, Sam Pope, 11, 15, 16, 17, 18, 19, 20, 21, 31, 32, 51, 54, 55, 78, 167
Brinkly, David, 36
British Broadcasting Corporation (BBC), 36, 37, 43, 69
Britt, George, 78, 159–60
Brown, Anthony Cave, 8
Brown, Ed, 46, 109
Bueiz, George, 24
Bulloch, John, 177–8
Burke, Don, 44
Burrows, Larry, 36, 50
Bustani, Emile, 46
Bustani, Myrna, 5, 9, 35, 107, 183–5, 187, 208
Byrn, Jimmy, 180

Casablanca, 11
Cavendish, Anthony, 10, 77, 192
Central Intelligence Agency (CIA), 3, 11, 17, 31, 36, 41, 45, 46, 47, 48, 49, 51, 55–6, 57, 63–4, 65, 76–7, 80, 84, 86–95, 97–105, 121, 148, 152–3, 159
Chamoun, President, 90, 102

211

INDEX

Chancellor, John, 10, 36, 38, 39, 45, 57–9, 63–4
Chehab, Farid, 152, 192
Clark, William, 47
Coca Cola, 180
Collins, Larry, 16, 18, 32, 36, 42, 54, 55
Columbia Broadcasting System (CBS), 11, 16, 37, 204
Cooke, Arthur, 167
Cooley, John, 43, 49
Copeland, Miles, 76, 81–2, 86, 152
Cuvellier, Nicole, 164–73, 186

Daily Express, 37
Daily Mail, 8, 20, 37, 43, 56, 149, 167
Daily Telegraph, 69, 177
Davis, Paul, 44, 50
de Mauney, Erik, 36, 37, 43
Delmer, Sefton, 5, 36, 37, 38, 56–7, 64, 76
Dimbleby, Jonathan, 36
Dreize, Judge, 170, 171, 172
Dreize, Maître, 171
Dulles, Allen, 82
Dweiri, Abdallah, 171, 172

E., J., 161
Economist, The, 20, 36, 41, 51, 76
Edde, Raymond, 7, 22, 23, 26, 32, 186, 205
Eden, Sir Anthony, 159
El Hout, Shafiq, 19, 25, 26, 28, 29, 30–1, 32
Ellender, Joseph, 21, 22, 32, 48, 118–21
Eveland, Wilbur Crane (Bill), 17, 18, 19, 21, 32, 75, 76, 86, 167, 195
Evening Standard, 114

Fahd, King, 48, 62–3, 64
Faisal, King, 22, 30, 48, 97, 115, 119, 130
Fayez, Akef Pasha Al, 26, 27, 29
First Casualty, The, 52
Fistere, John, 21, 23–4, 31, 32, 44, 80–1, 82, 86, 93, 146, 192, 193, 195
Fodor, Denis, 44, 49, 146
For Lust of Knowing, 153
Ford Motor Company, 124–5
Fortune, 4
Frazer, Blair, 36, 37, 38, 45

Gadafi, Muammar al-, 30, 121, 202
Gahtani, Farhan Al, 24–5, 30
Game of Nations, The, 76, 82
Getty, J. Paul, 5, 46, 109
Ghossun, Hanna, 26, 29, 32, 36, 39, 79, 107
Godley, C McMurtie, 205
Goodwin, Joe, 123
Gordon, Donald, 57, 58
Granselle, Cezar, 122, 123, 124
Great Britain, 148, 150, 153, 156, 192
Green, John, 164–5, 167, 170, 172–3
Griggs, Lee, 44
Guardian, 36, 50

Hammad, Kheiry, 25, 26, 28, 29, 32, 41, 42, 75–6, 91–3
Hammad, Suheil Abu, 54, 55
Hammerskjøld, Dag, 47
Hartwell, Lord, 177
Hawthorne, Mary, 186, 187
Heikal, Mohammed Hasanein, 19, 36, 77
Helms, Richard, 94
Holden, David, 40
Holloway, Admiral, 57–8
Hulac, Charles, 94
Hussein, King of Jordan, 18, 19, 21, 24, 29, 31, 33, 36, 42, 49, 53, 54–6, 63, 64, 65–70, 89, 91, 93, 130, 132–3, 136, 142, 145, 146, 155, 156–8
Hussein, Saddam, 30
Husseini, Haidar Al, 151, 153
Husseini, Haj Amin Al, 150–1, 152, 153
Hutchison, Robert, 93–4

Ibrahim, Fadya, 25
India, 53
Intra Bank, 111–12, 127–9
Iran, 122, 123, 202
Iraq, 21, 23, 29–30, 42, 43, 47, 48, 56, 76, 87–8, 113–14, 131, 149–50, 182–3
Iskander, Afifa, 181–3, 187
Israel, 57, 63, 124, 149, 157, 202
Ittayem, Fuad, 36
Izzard, Molly, 82
Izzard, Ralph, 20, 21, 32, 43, 80

Jennings, Peter, 36
Jerusalem, mufti of (Haj Amin Al Husseini), 150–1, 152, 153, 160

INDEX

Jordan, 23–4, 27, 44, 49, 57, 63, 65–6, 125, 132–3, 142–3, 145, 156
Jumblatt, Mai, 185, 187

Kallsen, Dick, 16, 79
Kassem, Abdel Karim, 21, 23, 29, 30, 47
Khalid, King, 62
Khalil, Abu, 9, 195, 205
Khashogi, Adnan, 45, 48
Kissinger, Henry, 206
Knightley, Philip, 52, 83
Kondakjian, Harry, 58, 164, 165, 175
Kurds, 43, 56–7
Kuwait, 47–8, 52
    Emir of, 127–8

Le Monde, 56
League of Arab States see Arab League
Lebanon, 6–7, 23, 32, 59, 201–2
Levine, Win, 73
Liberation Army, 149
Libya, 45
Luce, Henry, 36
Ludwig, Daniel, 5, 112

M., E., 155–9
M., G., 192
McHale, Bill, 84
MacLaughlin, Bill, 11, 37, 204, 205, 206
MacLintock, Robert, 77
Majali, Haza Pasha Al, 22, 141–2, 143–4, 145
Mecklin, John, 18–19, 20, 21, 24, 25, 26, 27, 29, 32, 44, 67, 69–70, 73, 157, 181
Mecklin, Shirley, 181, 187
Mecom, John, Sr, 25, 27, 29, 31
Metropolitan Museum of New York, 129–30
MI6, 10, 43, 46, 47, 51, 77, 105, 193
Middle East Airlines, 112, 116
Mohamad bin Abdul Aziz, Prince, 60
Mseitif, Mohammad, 9
Muamar, Abdul Aziz, 96–8
Muamar, Saud, 98
Muhammed, Crown Prince of Jordan, 142, 144, 146, 147
My Secret War, 81

N., M.S., 149–53
Nabulsi, Suleiman, 67
Nassar, Salim, 36

Nasser, Gamal Abdel, 6, 18, 19, 25, 29, 30, 32, 43, 49, 53, 54, 59, 65–9, 76, 88, 89, 130, 131–2, 155, 157–8, 159
Nasser bin Jamil, Sherrif, 57
National Broadcasting Company (NBC), 10, 16, 17, 37, 44, 58
Nawar, Ali Abu, 67
New York Times, 11, 15, 17, 18, 19, 31, 36, 38, 46, 51, 54, 55, 56
Newsday, 145
Newsweek, 36, 37, 44, 56
Nueiri, Omar, 84, 100, 101

Observer, 20, 36, 41, 51
Olayan, Suleiman, 45
Oldfield, Maurice, 77, 90, 94, 192
Orfally, Safa Eddine, 130–2
Organization of Petroleum-Exporting Countries (OPEC), 27, 59
Ottayem, Fuad, 60
Oweini, Hussein, 184
Owen, Garry, 121, 122

Palestine Liberation Organization (PLO), 19, 30, 127, 150, 207
Palestinians, 65
Parker, Paul, 10, 45, 107, 109, 112
Pay-Off, 50, 63
Philby, Eleanor, 11, 16, 21, 78, 79, 186
Philby, Kim, 3, 5, 11, 16, 20, 21, 23, 31, 32, 36, 41, 42, 51, 75–85, 86, 89, 96, 191–2, 195
Philby, St John, 11, 83
Pringle, Jim, 50

Qaddafi see Gadafi

Rahman, Kamel Abdel, 45
Radio Free Europe (RFE), 16, 28, 54
Randall, Jonathan, 37, 43, 46, 49, 204, 205–6
Riashi, Marc, 24, 36
Richards, Mr, 195
Rockefeller, David, 109
Roosevelt, Archie, 5, 33, 77, 86, 95, 151–2, 153
Roosevelt, Kate Tweedie, 178–9, 187
Roosevelt, Kim, 77, 95
Ropes of Sand, 17, 75
Russia, 43, 56–7, 76, 112

INDEX

S., A.R., 155
S., H., 160–2
Saïd, Abu *see* Aburish, Abu Saïd
Saïd, Nuri, 130, 149
Salam, Saeb, 58
Salameh, Abu Hassan, 207
Salha, Najib, 112
Saturday Evening Post, 81
Saud, King, 18, 22, 30, 43, 96
Saudi Arabia, 22, 26, 27, 28, 30, 36, 43,
    48, 60–1, 96–8, 115–16, 119, 122,
    190–1, 196
Scott, Gavin, 10, 33
Shaishakly, Adib, 130, 195–6
Shalan, Fawaz Al, 195
Shaker, Ghazi, 111
Sheehan, Edward R. F., 81–2
Slade-Baker, Col. John, 40, 41
Smith, Russ, 110
Solh, Khaldoun Es, 134, 203–4
Solh, Takkieddine Es, 203
Speechily, John, 114
Stewart, Desmond, 182
Streithorst, Nicole, 79
Streithorst, Tom, 16, 17, 18, 20, 22, 32,
    44, 79
Suez, 155–9
Sulzberger, C. L., 36, 37, 38
Sunday Times, 40, 83
Syria, 55, 149–50, 195, 201

T., A., 61–3
T., D.D., 193
Tallal, Prince, 43

Tariki, Abdallah, 26, 27–8, 30, 119–
    121
Taylor, Henry, Jr, 40, 41, 53–4, 55
Tibi, Afif Al, 26, 29, 32, 36
Time, 3, 10, 18, 19, 22, 25, 36, 37, 42, 44,
    49, 51, 55, 61, 62–3, 67–9, 70, 84, 93,
    146, 194
Times, The, 40
Touhy, Bill, 36
Toukan, T .wfiq, 135–7
Turkey, 194
Twal, Shehadeh, 124–5

United Arab Republic, 25, 29, 55
United Nations, 47
United Press International (UPI), 16, 36,
    42, 54
United States of America, 148, 150, 202

Wahab, Jamil Pasha Abdel, 21, 22, 23,
    29, 186
Walker, Hank, 36
Wallace, James, 18–19
Washington Post, 37, 43, 204, 206
West, Dame Rebecca, 177–8
Westland Helicopters, 113–14
Woman Besieged, A, 182
Worthington, Peter, 36
Wynn, Wilton, 81, 199

Yamani, Sheikh Zaki, 30
Young, Gavin, 36

Zeiback, Issa Selim Al, 23, 29, 30